# THE EPISTLE OF PAUL TO THE ROMANS

An Exposition

# THE EPISTLE
# OF PAUL
# TO THE ROMANS

## An Exposition

by
CHARLES R. ERDMAN

PREFACE BY EARL F. ZEIGLER

THE WESTMINSTER PRESS

PHILADELPHIA

Published by The Westminster Press®
Philadelphia, Pennsylvania

PRINTED IN THE UNITED STATES OF AMERICA

*To*
*my brother*
*Walter C. Erdman*
*an honored and beloved*
*herald of the gospel*
*in the Far East*

# PREFACE

Any writer who has been commissioned to prepare an exposition of Paul's letter to the Romans faces a challenging assignment. It is the longest of Paul's extant writings. It contains an extensive statement of his theological beliefs; and it is difficult reading in places. Some expositors say that the "Romans" to whom Paul was writing were largely slaves and freedmen, only recently emancipated from heathenism and pagan superstitions. This may have been true of the Gentile converts. The Jewish members obviously were not of this background. But whatever the mental capacity of his readers in Rome, Paul paid them the compliment of believing that they could understand what he wrote. And who are we to say that they could not? Our task is to read and comprehend this masterpiece of theological doctrine. And who are we to say that we cannot?

Incidentally, Paul came in for a bit of gentle chiding by the writer of II Peter 3:15-16 (italics mine) who said: "So also our beloved brother Paul wrote to you according to the wisdom given him, speaking of this as he does in all his letters. *There are some things in them hard to understand,* which the ignorant and unstable twist to their own destruction, as they do the other scriptures."

The letter to the Romans, although it requires the student to use his mind, has a tremendous appeal to one's desire to witness to the faith. Paul's irrepressible longing to visit the believers in the Imperial City was not the desire of a tourist for travel and sight-seeing. "I long to see you," he writes, "that I may impart some spiritual gift to strengthen you, that is, that we may be mutually encouraged by each other's faith." (Ch. 1:11-12.) And what was the essence of the gift? It was the apostle's gospel of which he was not ashamed. Dr. Erdman, the writer of the volume for which this preface is prepared, explains most helpfully what Paul meant by not being ashamed of the gospel. See expository notes for ch. 1:16-17. We cannot read what Paul has so aptly said without asking ourselves whether we can also affirm without mental or other reservations, "We are not ashamed of the gospel." Many "gospels" are being offered to the people of all nations during this revolutionary period of world history. Some of them make so strong an appeal that their followers will die for their ideologies. Christians believe, however, that there is, and always will be, but one *gospel* that is the power of God for salvation. That is the gospel so wonderfully set forth in the Romans. To read and understand Paul's exposition of this gospel is to be fired with a zeal to make it known to the last man and woman and child on the earth.

This volume entitled THE EPISTLE OF PAUL TO THE ROMANS is the skillful handiwork of Dr. Charles R. Erdman, also the expositor for each of the other sixteen volumes comprising the Erdman Commentaries on the complete New Testament. The continuing demand for this series over a period of many years attests to the satisfaction that users have expressed who have been under the tutelage of Dr. Erdman. These users have been pastors, church school teachers, college and seminary students, and the rank and file of the laity who demand rightly that they be given scholarly and evangelical guidance as they study.

The writer of this preface has no hesitancy in recommending with enthusiasm this volume by Dr. Erdman.

EARL F. ZEIGLER

# FOREWORD

The purpose of this brief exposition is to make a little more plain to modern readers the meaning and permanent values of a letter written by Saint Paul to certain residents of ancient Rome. Probably this epistle should be regarded as the supreme masterpiece of the great apostle. It is a marvel of intellectual acumen, of logical power, and of spiritual insight. However, it was first intended, not for the philosophers of the Imperial City, nor for the savants of the schools, nor for the circle of Caesar's household, but for the members of an infant Christian church, composed largely of slaves and freedmen, recently delivered from a degrading heathenism and from the bondage of pagan superstitions. Therefore, in spite of its depth and its difficulties, it has been bringing light and strength to persons of widely differing degrees of intelligence through all the succeeding centuries. To none has its guidance been more grateful than to those troubled by the problems and perplexities of modern thought; for the gospel of Christ, which it sets forth, is still the sweetest music ever heard upon earth, the most powerful message proclaimed among men, the most precious treasure entrusted to the people of God.

# INTRODUCTION

There is a thrilling significance in the simple statement of the date and authorship of this epistle. It was written in days when there were still living countless men and women who had walked and talked with Christ, and it was written by one who had become a close friend of the most intimate disciples of Christ. Its statements, therefore, reveal to us beyond question what Christianity was in its original form, and when it refers to the resurrection of Christ, to his redeeming work, to his deity, and to other familiar doctrines of the Christian faith, it assures us that our religion is not composed of myths or of uncertain traditions but rests on a firm basis of historic facts.

Paul was at Corinth. It was late in the winter of A.D. 57–58. For three years he had been laboring at Ephesus. It was that period of his life popularly known as his third missionary journey. On the first of these journeys, he had visited Cyprus and Southern Asia Minor. On the second, he had crossed to Europe and founded churches at Philippi, Thessalonica, and Corinth, and from this last city had written his two letters to the Thessalonians.

On this third journey, his long stay at Ephesus had been attended with great success. The gospel had been given to the entire province of Asia. He had written his important letter to the Galatians and his first epistle to the Corinthians and had formed a determination to preach the gospel at Rome. Before visiting the Imperial City, however, he had found it necessary first to return to Jerusalem and bring to the "poor among the saints" there an offering from the churches of Macedonia and Greece. To secure this offering and further to establish these churches, he had left Ephesus, journeying westward through Macedonia. There he had written his second letter to the Corinthians, to prepare that church for his approaching visit. Then, when he had reached Corinth and when his work in that city was about complete, as he was starting eastward on his long and perilous journey to Jerusalem, having in mind his determination to return westward and to visit Rome, he wrote this letter, to send messages to the Christian believers in the great capital, to assure them of his intended visit after he had accomplished his mission to Jerusalem, and to give them an orderly and comprehensive statement of the gospel of Christ.

It was natural that Paul, the apostle to the Gentiles, should wish to send a clear summary of the Christian faith to the church situated in the metropolis of the Gentile world. Further, he was planning to make Rome the point of departure for his work of evangelizing the western half of the Empire. He hoped that it would become the radiating center and permanent home of a universal activity which would bring to all nations the knowledge of Christ. Rome, too, was the emporium into which all peoples had poured their idolatries and corruptions, their lawlessness and their sin; it was a mirror of the heathen world, with its wretchedness and misery and its dread foreboding of the wrath to come. He wished, therefore, that in this city the good news of salvation should be proclaimed in all its fullness and its power; and he wrote this letter to encourage and to instruct the company of Christians upon whom in such large measure was to depend the evangelization of the world.

The origin of the church at Rome is lost in obscurity. Probably neither of the two most popular conjectures is correct. According to the former, it was founded by the "sojourners from Rome" who had heard the gospel message in Jerusalem on the Day of Pentecost. According to the latter, it was established by the preaching of the apostle Peter. Now, whether or not Peter ever visited the Imperial City, it is certain that this church was not of his planting; for Paul not only made no mention of him in this letter but, on the other hand, he distinctly stated that in coming to Rome he would "not build upon another man's foundation."

Nor is it probable that the Jews who had heard Peter preach in Jerusalem had returned to establish this church in Rome: for this was a Gentile church, and not until many years after Pentecost had believers learned that Gentiles as such could be admitted to the Christian church on equal terms with Jews. Probably the church had been founded by teachers or travelers from some of the Gentile centers by whom the universal character of the gospel was fully understood.

The church in Rome, however, evidently contained a large Jewish element, and it was in contact with a great Jewish community in the capital city. Some modern writers intimate that the church, in fact, was composed largely of Gentile Christians who had previously become proselytes to Judaism. However this may have been, the Jews were ever in the mind of Paul as he penned this epistle. Aside from his references to the Jews, the letter cannot be understood. Some churches, like those in Galatia, were in danger of undue Jewish influence; the church in the Gentile capital, however, was inclined to ignore the Jews, to forget the religious benefits they had brought to the race, to be blind to their history and indifferent to their future destiny. On the other hand, the Jews were tempted to boast their superior privileges and to place a false confidence on their relation to the Mosaic law. Therefore, Paul writes this letter, not merely to set forth the content of the gospel, but to do so with his own countrymen in mind, with the purpose of showing the relation of Jew and Gentile in the economy of God and of teaching that both were in need of the salvation which the gospel proclaimed and that both should be united harmoniously in one body, freed from all their former national prejudices, and living as a pattern and an example to believers of all nations.

The general line of argument is as follows: After a salutation in which Paul makes significant reference to the gospel (Rom. 1:1-7) and an expression of his interest in the Christians at Rome (vs. 8-15), he states definitely the theme of the epistle: "I am not ashamed of the gospel: for it is the power of God unto salvation to every one that believeth; to the Jew first, and also to the Greek. For therein is revealed a righteousness of God from faith unto faith: as it is written, But the righteous shall live by faith" (vs. 16-17).

He then shows that the whole world is in need of righteousness, whether lawless Gentiles (vs. 18-32) or privileged Jews (chs. 2:1 to 3:8); all, without exception, as the Jewish Scriptures declare, are guilty before God (ch. 3:9-20).

Paul then sets forth the nature of the righteousness which God graciously provides, in the redeeming work of Christ, for all who put their faith in him. (Vs. 21-31.)

He shows that this way of salvation is taught in the Old Testament Scriptures (ch. 4), that it results in peace and joy and hope (ch. 5:1-11), and that its benefits are universal to all who believe (vs. 12-21).

The apostle then shows how faith results in a life of holiness. He does so by answering three supposed objections to the doctrine of salvation by faith in Christ alone. The first of these objections is that one thus saved will be encouraged to sin. To this Paul replies that, on the contrary, faith involves such a union with the crucified and risen Christ as results in death to sin and in resurrection to a new moral life. (Ch. 6:1-14.)

The second objection is that this way of salvation makes one free to sin. The reply is that faith rather breaks the bondage of sin and results in the acceptance of a new obligation to holiness and in the enjoyment of a sanctifying oneness with Christ. (Chs. 6:15 to 7:6.)

In the third place, it is intimated that such a doctrine of salvation "apart from the law" makes the law a useless, even an evil, thing. To this Paul answers that the function of the law is not to relieve from sin, but to reveal sin, and that the reason it cannot save is not that it is evil but that man is sinful and weak. (Ch. 7:7-25.)

After answering these objections, Paul shows that faith in Christ and the consequent indwelling and operation of the Holy Spirit result in a life of holiness (ch. 8:1-11) as sons of God (vs. 12-17), and will issue in ultimate glory for believers who are meanwhile sustained by the Spirit and assured of the love of God (vs. 18-39).

The apostle reaches the climax of his discussion by considering the problem of how to reconcile the predictions of blessing upon the Jews, contained in their prophetic Scriptures, with their present rejection and condemnation. Paul answers, first, that the promises were only to the true Israel, to the "election," who really exercised faith (ch. 9:1-29); secondly, that the present rejection of Israel was not arbitrary, but was due to their refusal to accept the very way of salvation by faith taught in their own Scriptures (chs. 9:30 to 10:21); and, lastly, that the rejection of Israel is not final; even now some Jews are being saved, and in the future all will be saved, and with the Gentiles will trust in the Redeemer, Christ (ch. 11).

The remainder of the epistle is composed of exhortations to Christian living, based upon the great truths of saving grace previously set forth. These relate first to Christian duties in general. As members of the church, believers are to be unselfish (ch. 12); as citizens of the state, they are to show loyalty and submission (ch. 13:1-7); as members of society, they are to live in love and purity (ch. 13:8-14). More particularly, instruction is given as to conduct in relation to questions of conscientious scruples. Remembering the Lordship of Christ, believers are not to judge or to tempt one another but to exercise mutual forbearance, following the example of the Master. (Chs. 14:1 to 15:13.) The letter closes with paragraphs of personal explanations and greetings. (Chs. 15:14 to 16:27.)

# THE OUTLINE

## III

# I
# THE INTRODUCTION
## Rom. 1:1-17

## A. THE SALUTATION Ch. 1:1-7

*1 Paul, a servant of Jesus Christ, called to be an apostle, separated unto the gospel of God, 2 which he promised afore through his prophets in the holy scriptures, 3 concerning his Son, who was born of the seed of David according to the flesh, 4 who was declared to be the Son of God with power, according to the spirit of holiness, by the resurrection from the dead; even Jesus Christ our Lord, 5 through whom we received grace and apostleship, unto obedience of faith among all the nations, for his name's sake; 6 among whom are ye also, called to be Jesus Christ's: 7 to all that are in Rome, beloved of God, called to be saints: Grace to you and peace from God our Father and the Lord Jesus Christ.*

It required real genius so to phrase an opening salutation as to embody the substance of the epistle which followed. Such salutations were commonly mere conventional forms, like those with which modern letters are begun and ended; they designated the writer and the reader and included some word of greeting; Paul, however, used the opportunity to declare his authority as an apostle, to describe the Christians in Rome, and to define the gospel of which he was about to write.

As to himself, he said that he was "a servant of Jesus Christ, called to be an apostle, separated unto the gospel of God." These terms express startling claims, yet they imply privileges which belong to all who preach the good news, and even to all who are followers of Christ.

"A servant of Jesus Christ" is parallel to the Old Testament phrase, "a servant of Jehovah," and may intimate that Paul ventured to put himself in the place of the prophets and leaders of the Old Dispensation, while in a connection hitherto reserved for that of "Jehovah" he substituted the name of his Master, "Jesus Christ."

At least it is certain that Paul indicated here his complete submission to his Lord. The word "servant" means a "slave," a "bond servant." By its use Paul intimated that he had been purchased by his Master, and that he was surrendered wholly to his will. Such should be the relation to Christ realized by every one of his followers. It should be the complete submission and loving service of one who has been "bought with a price" and who "will not go out free."

The sphere of Paul's willing service was that of the apostleship. He did not number himself among the original Twelve, but he placed himself upon an equality with them and claimed all their high powers and privileges. Particularly, he insisted upon his apostolic authority. He declared that he was "called to be an apostle" or, more exactly, he was an apostle in consequence of a call. He may have had in mind the eternal purpose of God, or, quite as probably, the summons received from his risen Lord on the way to Damascus, or his subsequent commission to worldwide service. Surely Paul was ever sustained by the consciousness of a divine call; and in some real sense all who submit to the will of Christ may believe that he has a purpose in their experiences and in their tasks, and thus they may be patient to suffer and strong to serve.

As an "apostle" or messenger of Christ, Paul believed he had been entrusted with a special message, namely, "the gospel." He said that he had been "separated unto" this gospel; its proclamation was his sole task; this "one thing" and this alone he felt himself set aside to do, and his matchless success as a messenger of Christ has been, through all the Christian centuries, an inspiring example of concentration in effort and singleness of aim.

The word "gospel" means "good news" or "glad tidings"; and Paul has described it as "the gospel of God." That is, it has its source or origin in God; it is not an invention of man; it is a revelation, heavenly, glorious, divine.

This gospel God had "promised afore through his prophets in the holy scriptures"; they were "his prophets" and therefore guided, directed, inspired by him.    Their writings were "holy" because of their origin, their character, and their content.    In these "scriptures," now known as the Old Testament, the gospel was contained in type and symbol and prophecy; they foretold the great redemptive facts which were to form the substance of the gospel message.

Thus Paul not only introduced the theme of his epistle, but he outlined its main thought, namely that the good news of salvation by faith is no innovation, and that Christianity is not a contradiction of Judaism but its completion, its fulfillment, its climax.    The predicted Messiah of the Old Testament is the Christ of the New; the Servant of Jehovah whom the prophets predicted is the Son of God whom the apostles preached.

Thus Paul declared that "the gospel of God" was "concerning his Son," who is described as "born of the seed of David according to the flesh"; that is, in relation to the human race, in his physical being, in his earthly manifestation, he was of princely and royal lineage, even a son of Israel's greatest king, from whom the Messiah was promised to come; but, in his essential life, in his spirit of perfect and divine holiness, he "was declared to be the Son of God" by an act of supernatural power, namely, "by the resurrection from the dead," a resurrection which is so described as possibly to indicate that it is the pledge and assurance of the resurrection of those who put their trust in him, for the phrase might be translated, "By the resurrection of the dead."    In any case, Paul declared that the essence and sum and substance of the gospel is found in "Jesus Christ our Lord," in Jesus, the Messiah of the Jew, the Lord of the Christians.

Thus in a very real sense it is true that "Christianity is Christ." Unlike the Mohammedan or the Buddhist or the adherent of any other faith, the Christian centers his religion in the person and work and present power of his divine and loving Lord. It was from this risen Lord, Paul declared, that he himself had received saving grace, and the further favor of being appointed as a chosen apostle and messenger with a view to securing among all nations, among Gentiles as well as among Jews, that obedience and devotion to Christ which are of the very essence of faith. As the ultimate purpose of the gospel and of Paul's apostleship was to make more fully known the grace and glory and power of Christ, it was all "for his name's sake."

The readers to whom this epistle, with its exposition of the gospel, is being written, are described as residents of Rome and as belonging to the Gentile nations rather than to the Jews. This, however, does not mean that there were no Jews among them; in fact, Jewish converts must have formed a large element in the church; and throughout the whole epistle the Jew is constantly in mind.

However, whether Jews or Gentiles, all are comprehended in three luminous phrases. First, they are "called to be Jesus Christ's," that is, they belong to him and are his in response to a call. This call was quite as real and as sacred as that by which Paul was summoned to his apostolic service. Second, they are "beloved of God" as those who have been shown his saving mercy and have been brought into living fellowship with him through Jesus Christ. Third, they are "called to be saints"; that is, they are saints as a result of the divine call which made them followers and servants of Christ. The word "saints" denotes those who are separated from sin and separated unto God. They belong to God, like Israel of old, as his own peculiar people. They should feel obligated, therefore, to live in keeping with such a high calling; they "should be holy" as he who has called them is holy. Thus, "saints" is a term which expresses an ideal. In the New Testament, individual Christians are not called "saints." It is a word employed to denote communities of believers or the whole body of Christians, redeemed, sanctified, and expected to grow into the likeness of their Lord and Master.

To such believers Paul sent his usual salutation: "Grace to you and peace from God our Father and the Lord Jesus Christ." Grace is the source and peace the essence of that blessedness which believers enjoy. "Grace" was the common salutation among the Greeks, and "Peace" among the Jews; Paul combined them and deepened their meaning as he adopted them as his usual form of Christian greeting. "Grace" denotes the unmerited favor of God, and "Peace," both harmony with God and the peace of soul which ensues. This blessedness is bestowed by God himself whom, as Christians, we have learned to call "our Father," and from Jesus Christ whom, as the connection of words denotes, we have come to regard as one with the Father, our divine Savior and Lord.

## B. THE INTEREST OF PAUL IN THE ROMAN CHRISTIANS Ch. 1:8-15

*8 First, I thank my God through Jesus Christ for you all, that your faith is proclaimed throughout the whole world. 9 For God is my witness, whom I serve in my spirit in the gospel of his Son, how unceasingly I make mention of you, always in my prayers 10 making request, if by any means now at length I may be prospered by the will of God to come unto you. 11 For I long to see you, that I may impart unto you some spiritual gift, to the end ye may be established; 12 that is, that I with you may be comforted in you, each of us by the other's faith, both yours and mine. 13 And I would not have you ignorant, brethren, that oftentimes I purposed to come unto you (and was hindered hitherto), that I might have some fruit*

*in you also, even as in the rest of the Gentiles. 14 I am*
*debtor both to Greeks and to Barbarians, both to the wise*
*and to the foolish. 15 So, as much as in me is, I am ready*
*to preach the gospel to you also that are in Rome.*

In beginning his epistles, Paul usually added to the
formal salutation a thanksgiving and a prayer. Both of
these are found here, and both of them express the intense interest felt by Paul in the Christians at Rome to
whom the letter is addressed, an interest which deepened
his desire to preach the gospel of Christ in the great cen-
tral city of the world. "First, I thank my God"—even to
detach this phrase is to state a precious truth. "First, I
thank my God"—and when one thus begins a letter, a
day, a prayer, the bitterness disappears, the clouds drift
away, the burden is gone. "I thank my God through
Jesus Christ," writes the apostle, for it is only in virtue of
Jesus Christ, in view of all he is as the divine Mediator and
as the Way to the Father, that one draws near to God
in thanksgiving and prayer, and enjoys that holy intimacy
expressed by Paul when he uses the phrase "my God."
Such a sense of personal fellowship, such a consciousness
of the love of God toward us as individuals should be experienced by all who come unto God "through Jesus
Christ."

The reason why Paul returns thanks is the fact that
wherever he goes throughout the Empire or, as he says,
"throughout the whole world," word reaches him concerning the faith of the believers in Rome, and concerning
the wide influence they are exerting; for while it is always
a joy to a Christian worker to learn of the progress of the
gospel in distant lands, that joy is particularly great when
the tidings relate to missionary success in such a strategic
center as that of the capital city.

Paul rejoices in such tidings from the Roman Christians
because they are continually in his thoughts, his plans, and
his prayers. The One who can attest this interest is God

himself, to whom Paul renders service with the spiritual adoration of a worshiper, a service which finds its outward expression in his proclamation of the gospel of the Son of God.

The chief burden of his ceaseless prayer, as Paul declares, is the request that soon, after many previous delays, the Lord will make it possible for him to visit these friends in Rome. Paul does not hesitate to make specific petitions for definite objects; yet, as here, he accompanies the request by the submissive "if" of Christian faith, "if" it may be "the will of God."

How earnestly he desires to visit this infant church is expressed by the words, "I long to see you," I am heartsick with yearning, I am heartsick at delay. It is this longing which has made him pray so continually, and this longing has been caused by his desire to impart to those believers "some spiritual gift"—that is, some new development of spiritual life and light, some fuller understanding of the truth, some larger apprehension of the grace that is in Christ Jesus, "to the end" that in their Christian faith and hope they more fully "may be established."

However, Paul at once adds, with equal delicacy and tact and sincerity, that he yearns for such a visit not only because of the good he would give but also because of the good he would receive, because he would be "comforted" by their mutual faith. He realized what every minister of Christ has found true, that in imparting spiritual gifts of comfort and guidance and hope one's own soul is immeasurably enriched.

That the Romans themselves had been expecting such a visit, this whole section implies. That an explanation was due them for a further delay seems also to be indicated. They lived in the capital of the Gentile world; Paul was the official apostle to the Gentiles; once before he had come as far west as Corinth and had failed to pass on to Rome; now again he was at the Greek metropolis and was turning back toward the East with a gift for the Jewish

believers in Jerusalem; surely some message must be sent
to the Roman Christians, some explanation must be given
for a further delay in visiting them.

Therefore Paul employs one of his most emphatic and
characteristic phrases to introduce the statement that this
delay is due to no lack of desire on his part: "I would not
have you ignorant, brethren," writes Paul to make the following words more impressive, "oftentimes I purposed to
come unto you (and was hindered hitherto)." His purpose had been steadfast, but circumstances were beyond
his control. Duties may not conflict, but desires for service often do. He really yearned to "have some fruit"
among these Roman Christians, to serve them and others
through them, quite as much as among other Gentiles;
and he had formed a very definite plan of visiting Rome
and of passing on through Rome far westward to Spain.
Ultimately his desire and theirs was fulfilled; finally he
did reach the Imperial City, but in a way quite different
from his plan; he came not as a free herald of the truth,
passing triumphantly on to new fields of service, but as a
prisoner, bound with chains, to answer for his life before
the judgment seat of Caesar. His path lay through tumult
and prison and storm and shipwreck; yet this was the way
of Providence; it was thus that his own purpose was fulfilled, according to the will of God.

How earnest that purpose was, he now states with something of vehemence. His desire to come to Rome is not
merely to impart a gift; it is actually to pay a debt: "I am
debtor both to Greeks and to Barbarians, both to the wise
and to the foolish." By the term "Greeks" was denoted
all those peoples who, like the Greek and Roman, understood the language and shared the civilization commonly
classed as Hellenic or Greek, and were contrasted with
the comparatively uncivilized peoples and tongues outside
the molding influence of the "Greek." By the "wise"
were meant those inner circles of the educated and cultured who were familiar with the literature and philosophy

of the day, in contrast with the great "unthinking" masses who because of their ignorance and lack of education would be despised by the cultured classes of the Roman world. Paul meant to affirm that he felt under a solemn obligation to give to men of all races and classes and degrees of culture the gospel which had been committed to him as a sacred trust. Nor should any Christian look out upon the peoples of the world in any other light. Those unnumbered millions whom we call "heathen" or "pagan" or "Christless" are our creditors and to them we owe the glorious gospel which God has entrusted to us. To proclaim this gospel in all the world and to every creature is not a matter of sentiment or of choice; it is a moral obligation; it is a sacred duty.

Under the solemn compulsion of such a debt Paul declares: "So, as much as in me is, I am ready to preach the gospel to you also that are in Rome." He is saying that he is ready, he is prepared, he is eager; if there is any delay, it is no fault of his, no lack of desire on his part, but it is due to his circumstances and not to his choice. For the present, God had for Paul other fields of labor, but the delay was wisely ordered; it resulted in the writing of this epistle, which has been called "the chief book of the New Testament and the perfect gospel."

## C. THE THEME OF THE EPISTLE Ch. 1:16-17

*16 For I am not ashamed of the gospel: for it is the power of God unto salvation to every one that believeth; to the Jew first, and also to the Greek. 17 For therein is revealed a righteousness of God from faith unto faith: as it is written, But the righteous shall live by faith.*

In beginning his letter, Paul has been assuring his readers, the Christians at Rome, of his deep interest in them and of his earnest desire to visit them and to preach among them the gospel of Christ. He now states the supreme source of this desire. It is found in his love for the gospel and in his confidence in its saving power.

"I am not ashamed of the gospel," writes the apostle, and possibly he means that he is proud of the gospel. A negative statement is sometimes the most emphatic way of expressing an implied opposite, as for instance "not far from the kingdom" means "very near to the kingdom" and "no mean city" denotes a famous and prominent city. So here, when Paul writes that he is "not ashamed of the gospel" he may intend to say that he rejoices in the gospel and glories in the gospel.

On the other hand, there were reasons why the gospel might have been regarded as a cause of shame. Paul remembered how he had suffered for the gospel at Ephesus and at Philippi and at Corinth. He knew how foolish, to the wise men of the world, seemed that story of salvation through faith in a crucified Christ; and now, because of his long delay in proclaiming that message in mighty Rome, the center and symbol of imperial power and pomp and pride, it might be supposed that his delay was due to timidity or fear lest the gospel might seem to be an impotent and ineffectual thing in that great capital where all the forces of the world were centered and combined.

On the contrary, Paul declares that he is not ashamed of that gospel. Whatever may have occasioned his delay in visiting Rome, it has not been due to any fear on his part. He does realize the difficulties of the situation and the obstacles which will oppose him; his purpose is no jaunty and lighthearted plan of adventure; nevertheless he has no fear, no reluctance, no shame. He knows that the gospel is "the power of God unto salvation."

Thus, whether his statement that he is "not ashamed of the gospel" expressed Paul's pride or his lack of shame, in either case it serves to introduce the great theme of his epistle, namely, "the gospel" as "the power of God unto salvation," the revelation of the "righteousness" which is "by faith."

The gospel is thus defined in terms of "power"; it can do something; it is not a mere ornament, not simply a pleasing story, not only an interesting system of philosophy. It is "the power of God"; it can therefore do anything. It is "the power of God unto salvation"; it can therefore do everything the human soul needs for time and for eternity. It is "to every one that believeth"; it can do everything that is needed for everyone.

Thus Paul states the nature, the result, the freeness, and the universality of the gospel. It is designed to bring salvation to everyone who believes in Christ. This last idea Paul emphasizes by adding "to the Jew first, and also to the Greek." Here the term "Greek" is intended to denote the whole Gentile world in contrast with the Jew. Salvation is proclaimed for the Jew "first," not only in time, but by way of eminence. The Scriptures are his, the promises are his, the Christ is his "according to the flesh." However, no Jew can be saved aside from faith in Christ, and by faith in Christ any Gentile can be saved. This familiar but inexhaustible word "salvation" may be interpreted in terms of deliverance from sin, or of new spiritual life and soundness of soul. It denotes deliverance from the guilt of sin, granted to those who are "justified"; and deliverance from the power of sin, experienced by those who are being "sanctified"; and deliverance from the very presence and results of sin, enjoyed by those who are "glorified." Thus "salvation" may be regarded as past or present or future; in the first aspect, this theme is expanded in the opening five chapters of this letter. In the second and third aspects, it is developed in the sixth and seventh and eighth chapters. However, as a life of holiness and service, "salvation" is set forth in the closing or "practical" portion of the epistle. Thus in the widest use of the term, "salvation" may be interpreted to include all that a believer receives through faith in Christ, from the time he is pardoned as a penitent sinner until he realizes his fullest blessedness in eternal glory.

Paul further explains that the power of the gospel is due to the fact that "therein is revealed a righteousness of God from faith unto faith." One may note the importance to the argument of the little word "for." Paul desires to preach in Rome, "for" he is not ashamed of the gospel; and he is not ashamed of the gospel "for" it is "the power of God"; and it is the power of God "for" it reveals "a righteousness of God" which is "from faith unto faith."

The phrase "righteousness of God" as used in this particular verse does not refer to God's justice or to any of his attributes; nor yet does it denote the moral character wrought in man by the Spirit of God, but rather, that right relation to the requirements of divine law which God provides for those who trust in Christ. It signifies the acceptance granted to sinful man by a holy God. It is provided in and through Christ, and denotes God's way of justifying the unrighteous, God's method of liberating his love while vindicating his law.

As an old Puritan quaintly defined it, "The righteousness of God is that righteousness which God's righteousness requires him to require"; that is, an infinitely holy God can require of man nothing less than perfect righteousness, but as man cannot attain this by himself, God provides it for him through faith in Christ. Or, as another has expressed it, "The righteousness of God is the sum total of all that God commands, demands, approves, and himself provides through Jesus Christ."

God is therefore the Source, or the Giver, of this righteousness; man cannot attain or achieve it; he accepts it as a free gift by faith alone. It is "a righteousness of God from faith unto faith"; that is, it is of faith, first and last and wholly.

However, faith is not the mere intellectual acceptance of a truth; it expresses a relation to a divine Person, an attitude of trust and submission and love. That such an attitude of heart and mind brings one into right relation to God is no new truth. "Justification by faith" has been always the divine way of dealing with man, and therefore to attest the correctness of his great theme and to show the Jew that the gospel is in perfect accord with the teachings of the Old Testament, Paul closes with a familiar quotation from Habakkuk: "But the righteous shall live by faith." The old patriot and prophet whose words are thus quoted was pleading with Judah to trust in Jehovah and to obey him; and Paul intimates that the principle involved is permanent. The condition of receiving divine help is the same today as it was of old. The only hope for the men of Judah was to live by faith; and so, since God has revealed his redeeming love in Jesus Christ, the one who puts his trust in that Savior is accepted of God, he possesses the "righteousness of God," he is justified by faith; for "the righteous shall live by faith."

No wonder that Paul was eager to preach a gospel which revealed so gloriously God's way of salvation, and no wonder that the expansion of this theme resulted in what may be regarded as the masterpiece among all his epistles.

# II
# DOCTRINAL INSTRUCTIONS
Chs. 1:18 to 11:36

## A. JUSTIFICATION BY FAITH
Chs. 1:18 to 5:21

### 1. THE UNIVERSAL NEED OF RIGHTEOUSNESS
Chs. 1:18 to 3:20

When Paul has stated the great theme of his epistle to be the righteousness which the gospel reveals, and which God provides for believers in Christ, he naturally begins his discussion by showing how universally and desperately such righteousness is needed by the human race. He first dwells upon the need of the Gentile nations and then of the Jews, and thus concludes that all men have sinned and are under the condemnation of God. Or, as logically arranged, the contents of this section (chs. 1:18 to 3:20) have been stated as follows:

Whosoever sins incurs the judgment of God from which he can be delivered only by the righteousness of God (ch. 2:1-16). But the heathen, although taught by nature and conscience (ch. 1:18-32), and the Jews, although possessing the Mosaic law (chs. 2:17 to 3:8), have sinned by falling short of, or contradicting, their respective standards of righteousness. Therefore, as the Old Testament had already proclaimed, the whole world is under the judgment of God and accordingly needs his righteousness (ch. 3:9-20).

### a. The Guilt of the Gentile World    Ch. 1:18-32

*18 For the wrath of God is revealed from heaven against all ungodliness and unrighteousness of men, who hinder the truth in unrighteousness; 19 because that which is known of God is manifest in them; for God manifested it unto them. 20 For the invisible things of him since the creation of the world are clearly seen, being perceived through the things that are made, even his everlasting power and divinity; that they may be without excuse: 21 because that, knowing God, they glorified him not as God, neither gave thanks; but became vain in their reasonings, and their senseless heart was darkened. 22 Professing themselves to be wise, they became fools, 23 and changed the glory of the incorruptible God for the likeness of an image of corruptible man, and of birds, and four-footed beasts, and creeping things.*

*24 Wherefore God gave them up in the lusts of their hearts unto uncleanness, that their bodies should be dishonored among themselves: 25 for that they exchanged the truth of God for a lie, and worshipped and served the creature rather than the Creator, who is blessed for ever. Amen.*

*26 For this cause God gave them up unto vile passions: for their women changed the natural use into that which is against nature: 27 and likewise also the men, leaving the natural use of the woman, burned in their lust one toward another, men with men working unseemliness, and receiving in themselves that recompense of their error which was due.*

*28 And even as they refused to have God in their knowledge, God gave them up unto a reprobate mind, to do those things which are not fitting; 29 being filled with all unrighteousness, wickedness, covetousness, maliciousness; full of envy, murder, strife, deceit, malignity; whisperers, 30 backbiters, hateful to God, insolent, haughty, boastful, inventors of evil things, disobedient to parents, 31 without understanding, covenant-breakers, without natural affection, unmerciful: 32 who, knowing the ordinance of God, that they that practise such things are worthy of death, not only do the same, but also consent with them that practise them.*

This dark and painful picture of the pagan world is only the more distressing when we remember that it is painted in even more revolting detail by the classical writers of the Roman world.

It is a picture of the degradation into which mankind ever sinks when turning from the truth of God and no longer restrained by his grace.

It was given as the reason why Paul gloried in the gospel and desired to have it proclaimed in Rome. It should arouse all Christian readers today to hasten the preaching of this gospel as the only hope of the human race. The entire passage (vs. 18-32) is summarized in verse 18, which states: (1) that the truth as to God has been manifest to men (vs. 19-20); (2) that by them it has been hindered or repelled (vs. 21-23); and (3) that consequently the wrath of God has been revealed as resting upon them (vs. 24-32).

"The wrath of God" is a phrase which easily may be misunderstood. It must not be associated with any ideas of human passion or frailty or revenge. It must not make us unmindful of the universal love of God. It is in fact the reverse side of his love. It is the attitude against sin which a holy God must take as he sees how sin wounds and tortures and destroys the creatures who are the special objects of his care. God loves the sinner, but he hates and punishes sin.

His wrath "is revealed," not in the gospel alone or by any supernatural act but by what history shows of the degradation which results from sin, and the universal conviction of the race that sin is inevitably punished by pain and misery and death. This revelation is "from heaven," the dwelling place and throne of God; by which is meant that this inseparable relation between sin and punishment is a divine arrangement. It operates as a natural law, but it is in accordance with a divinely established order.

This condemnation of God is revealed "against all ungodliness and unrighteousness of men"; that is, against all impiety, or all failures in the religious sphere, and against all injustice, or all failures in the moral sphere. This distinction is kept up through the remainder of the chapter, where the apostle pictures first the impiety and then the immorality of the heathen world.

Both these forms of guilt are due to the fact that men are refusing to live in accordance with the light given them. They sinfully "hinder the truth"; they repress it, they hold it down or hold it back, so that it is not allowed to produce its natural effect upon moral conduct. This truth is none other than the truth concerning God, and so concerning right and duty.

(1) The truth has been manifested both in the light of conscience and by the witness of external nature (vs. 19-20). "That which is known of God," without the revelation in Christ, is revealed in the hearts and minds of men. This revelation is imparted by God himself, and it is mentally discerned by reflecting upon his works. These display his "everlasting power and divinity." Probably the first impression which nature gives is that of power; it speaks to a thoughtful mind of a First Cause, of an unseen Creator, whose power is limitless; yet it also speaks of his "divinity," that is, of his other perfections, his wisdom and his goodness. The very world itself is described by the word "cosmos," which means "order," and which argues for design on the part of the Maker. Then, too, as a closer knowledge of the world points back the mind to vistas of uncounted ages, one naturally concludes that the creative Power is "everlasting," eternal; and the attributes thus revealed in nature all testify that this eternal Power is a divine Person. Thus arguing from "cause and effect," from "design," from "order," and from "being," man finds in external nature that real knowledge of God which the voice of conscience confirms. Possibly Christians do not always appreciate natural religion as fully as they should. It gives such a true revelation of God that men have no excuse for either impiety or injustice. In fact, its very design is "that they may be without excuse." This startling statement, however, must be interpreted to mean merely

that in case man fell into error as to belief or conduct, the fault would be wholly his own.

(2) As a matter of fact, this truth has been hindered and repelled and corrupted and lost (vs. 21-23). Paul here states the important and practical principle that religious knowledge unless acted upon never can be retained. He traces the steps by which the heathen world descended from a knowledge of the true God to the most degraded and ignorant idolatry; and it is possible even today for men to move in the same direction.

First, there was indifference to God. Knowing him, they neither praised him for his perfections nor thanked him for his goodness: "They glorified him not as God, neither gave thanks."

Then, they "became vain in their reasonings," for nothing can be more ridiculous than the religious speculations of irreligious men. Those who refuse to worship God, and who do not love to obey him are often the authors of theories and mistaken beliefs as popular as they are "empty" and absurd.

Then, they totally forgot God. "Their senseless heart was darkened." The whole inner being, deprived of a knowledge of truth and holiness and right, became wholly corrupted.

The next state which resulted was that of intellectual pride coexisting with spiritual and moral folly. "Professing themselves to be wise, they became fools." (V. 22.) Such, in view of their spiritual impotence and their inability to keep men from moral corruption, is the divine estimate of the proudest philosophers of Greece and of Rome, and of all the boasted wisdom of the Euphrates and the Nile. Even today the blindest infidelity is coincident with the most insufferable conceit. The modern wise man worships himself. The folly of the ancient world manifested itself in gross forms of idolatry. This was the last stage in religious degeneracy: "They . . . changed the glory of the incorruptible God for the likeness of an image of cor-

ruptible man, and of birds, and four-footed beasts, and
creeping things." The odiousness of idolatry is not only
in its resultant immorality but in that it caricatures and
slanders God. It does not stop in likening him to a man,
but it figures him as a bird, a beast, or a reptile, and
teaches men to offer divine worship to the most foul and
repulsive forms.

Such is Paul's startling review of the religious history of
the race. Beginning with the worship of the living and
true God, mankind gradually descended to idolatry and
fetishism. The development has not been upward but
downward. Paganism has no saving power in itself. The
only hope for the world lies in the gospel of Christ.

(3) Finally, Paul shows how "the wrath of God" has
been revealed (vs. 24-32). It has been manifested in his
abandonment of the heathen to the consequences of their
guilt. They willfully turned from him, and became worshipers of idols, and he therefore allowed them to suffer
the inevitable result of an ever-deepening moral degradation.

In this degeneration, Paul notes three stages, each one
marked by the statement, "God gave them up" (vs. 24,
26, 28).

First of all, he "gave them up . . . unto uncleanness."
They were allowed to be swept by the strong currents of
their impure desires down into the abyss of immorality and
vice; and this because they chose to worship "the creature rather than the Creator," the ever-blessed God.
(Vs. 24-25.)

Thus Paul intimates that morality depends upon religion, and cannot endure long without the sanctions of
religion. Nor can anyone today neglect the worship of
God without falling into the peril of evil thoughts and impure desires.

Secondly, "God gave them up unto vile passions."
They became the victims of the most abnormal lusts and
the most degrading vices. (Vs. 26-27.) All the abomina-

tions to which Paul refers are said to be fully corroborated by the heathen writers of his day. Their very statements emphasize the truths that sin brings its own punishment in the form of more shameful sins and that the yielding to wrong desire always results in bondage to passions even more perverse and "vile."

Lastly, Paul declares, "God gave them up unto a reprobate mind," a mind in which the distinctions between right and wrong are confused or lost, a mind upon which the disapproval of God cannot fail to rest. Such an inner disposition cannot fail to express itself in "things which are not fitting," which cannot be thought to be suitable or right. Of these Paul gives some twenty-one examples, and reaches the climax of his terrible indictment in the statement that those guilty of these crimes commit them with the full knowledge of the penalty of death which they deserve, and, worst of all, they rejoice in others, and encourage others, who practice the same sins.

This willful impurity, springing from defiant impiety, forms together with it a more melancholy and vivid and detailed picture of the universal depravity of the heathen world than Paul furnishes in any other portion of his epistles.

Is it not true that the elements of this picture are reproduced in all quarters of the world today? Was there not need, and is there not need, of that righteousness which God graciously provides for all through the Savior, Jesus Christ his Son?

### b. The Principles of Divine Judgment    Ch. 2:1-16

*1 Wherefore thou art without excuse, O man, whosoever thou art that judgest: for wherein thou judgest another, thou condemnest thyself; for thou that judgest dost practise the same things. 2 And we know that the judgment of God is according to truth against them that practise such things. 3 And reckonest thou this, O man, who judgest them that practise such things, and doest the same, that thou shalt escape the judgment of God? 4 Or despisest thou the riches of his goodness and forbearance and long-suffering, not knowing that the goodness of God leadeth thee to repentance? 5 but after thy hardness and impenitent heart treasurest up for thyself wrath in the day of wrath and revelation of the righteous judgment of God; 6 who will render to every man according to his works: 7 to them that by patience in well-doing seek for glory and honor and incorruption, eternal life: 8 but unto them that are factious, and obey not the truth, but obey unrighteousness, shall be wrath and indignation, 9 tribulation and anguish, upon every soul of man that worketh evil, of the Jew first, and also of the Greek; 10 but glory and honor and peace to every man that worketh good, to the Jew first, and also to the Greek: 11 for there is no respect of persons with God. 12 For as many as have sinned without the law shall also perish without the law: and as many as have sinned under the law shall be judged by the law; 13 for not the hearers of the law are just before God, but the doers of the law shall be justified; 14 (for when Gentiles that have not the law do by nature the things of the law, these, not having the law, are the law unto themselves; 15 in that they show the work of the law written in their hearts, their conscience bearing witness therewith, and their thought one with another accusing or else excusing* them); *16 in the day when God shall judge the secrets of men, according to my gospel, by Jesus Christ.*

A large part of the religion of some men seems to consist in their readiness to find fault with others. Such was the case of the Jew whom Paul here describes. In the midst of the flood of Gentile pollution and iniquities, which Paul has pictured in the preceding chapter, he sees one who, like a judge, from the heights of his tribunal, sends a stern look over the corrupt mass, condemning the evil which pervades it and applauding the wrath of God which punishes it. The man is not named, however, until Paul proceeds (vs. 17-29) to set forth the guilt and condemnation of the Jew. Meanwhile Paul sets forth the fact of divine judgment and its two great principles. (Ch. 2:1-16.)

(1) The fact of divine judgment is here stated in view of the sins of the heathen world and of the condemnation of them by the Jew. "And we know that the judgment of God is according to truth against them that practise such things." This is really a statement of the fundamental fact underlying the opening chapters of the epistle. (Chs. 1:18 to 3:20.) Whosoever sins incurs the condemnation of God, he here declares; but the Gentiles have sinned (ch. 1:18-32) and the Jews have sinned (chs. 2:17 to 3:8); therefore the whole world is guilty and in need of the righteousness which God provides (ch. 3:9-20).

To the fact of the inevitable punishment of sin, conscience is a witness. This is what Paul means as he addresses the one who is criticizing the Gentile world. "Wherefore thou art without excuse, O man, whosoever thou art that judgest: for wherein thou judgest another, thou condemnest thyself; for thou that judgest dost practise the same things." (Ch. 2:1.) The criticism of others shows that one has a conscience, but if he has a conscience by which he condemns his fellowmen, he should be guided by that conscience himself. The deceitfulness of the human heart is strikingly exhibited in the different judgments which men place on themselves and others, condemning in others what they excuse in themselves. Not infrequently the most censorious are the most guilty. Men commonly observe in others the faults which exist in themelves.

So, too, those who are most censorious of others seem to imagine that they will be judged by some other rule and thus escape the condemnation of God. At least, Paul so intimated in reference to the Jew: "And we know that the judgment of God is according to truth against them that practise such things. And reckonest thou this, O man, who judgest them that practise such things, and doest the same, that thou shalt escape the judgment of God?" (Vs.

2-3.) The Jew seems to have supposed that he occupied a privileged position. He imagined that in some way he could escape the judgment which was coming upon the Gentile, whereas in reality, this judgment would be "according to truth," that is, in accordance with guilt, with facts, and with desert.

Then, again, the Jew was falsely interpreting the very mercy of God. He was despising it as merely good-natured indifference to sin: "Or despisest thou the riches of his goodness and forbearance and longsuffering, not knowing that the goodness of God leadeth thee to repentance?" (V. 4.) Toward the Jews, God had shown peculiar goodness and patience and forbearance. They had misunderstood his purpose, which was to incline them to forsake their sins; instead, by their hardness and impenitence of heart, they had treasured up for themselves "wrath in the day of wrath and revelation of the righteous judgment of God" (v. 5).

There is to be such a day of retribution and punishment, a day when God's opposition to disobedience and sin must be manifested against sinners. This fact the universal conscience of mankind attests.

(2) The principles of such judgment, however, will be absolutely just: (a) Each man will be judged according to his deeds (vs. 6-11), and (b) each man will be judged according to his light (vs. 12-16).

Thus God, as Paul continues to affirm, (a) "will render to every man according to his works." The final awards of God are to be not according to a man's profession; the Jew thought that he might escape because he had Abraham as his father. Nor are these awards to be according to man's relations in life; the Jew thought that he was secure because he belonged to the chosen race and was thus an heir of the Kingdom. God is to award to every man according to his conduct; for, as Paul asserts in his climax, "there is no respect of persons with God" (v. 11). The intervening verses are an impressive enlargement and ap-

plication of this principle, that judgment will be according
to conduct. To those whose rule in life is to persevere in
doing good, whose object in life is to obtain hereafter a
glorious, honored, imperishable existence, God will give
"eternal life," a reward which does not mean merely an
endless continuance of existence, but a kind of existence,
life in its fullness, a life of blessedness, a life of glory.

On the other hand, to those who belong to the class of
selfish intriguers, whose motive is not "the truth" but immorality, there will be God's anger in its tranquil, judicial
form of "wrath," and in its outward self-manifestation of
"indignation."

Then, in reverse order, Paul emphatically repeats his
statements as to God's judging men according to their
works. There will be outward calamity and inward anguish upon every soul belonging to a man who brings evil
to pass, "of the Jew first, and also of the Greek"; but there
will be radiance of glory, honor, and eternal repose to
every man who works at what is good, "to the Jew first,
and also to the Greek."

Of course it is needless here to raise the question as to
whether this passage teaches salvation by works instead
of by faith. The words must be read in connection with
the chapters of the epistle of which they are a part. Suffice
it to say that one who does so "seek for glory and honor
and incorruption" will naturally accept the way which
God provides through Jesus Christ, and only through faith
will any man be able to attain that righteousness which
God requires. This, however, is a thought aside from
Paul's immediate argument. His emphatic statement here
is to the effect that the regular judgment of God will be
according to the conduct and the deeds of men.

(b) The judgment of God will be also according to the
light which each one severally has enjoyed. (Vs. 12-16.)
This is a further proof of the justice of God (v. 11), for,
as the ground of judgment is to be "works," so the rule of
judgment is to be light: "For as many as have sinned with-

out the law shall also perish without the law: and as many
as have sinned under the law shall be judged by the law"
(v. 12).  That is, the heathen who have sinned without
the advantage of the Mosaic law will perish also by the
sentence of God, as being unfaithful to the light of nature
but without any reference to the Mosaic law; and the Jews,
who have sinned in the midst of a system of revealed law,
will be judged by this law as if it were the author of their
condemnation.

Thus sin is the cause of death—not election or predestination, not lack of knowledge or ignorance of Christ, but
voluntary, willful sin, disobedience to law, unfaithfulness
to light, will occasion "death."  The word "perish" finds
its contrasts in such statements as "salvation" (ch. 1:16);
"shall live" (ch. 1:17); "eternal life" (ch. 2:7); "glory"
(ch. 2:10).  It is further contrasted with the word
"judged" in the same verse.  The heathen shall perish as
the natural consequence of their moral corruption.  The
Jews, and all who have enjoyed a clear and positive revelation of the will of God, will be subjected to a detailed in-
quiry such as arises from applying the particular articles
of a code.  The Jews, therefore, instead of occupying a
privileged position because of their familiarity with the
Mosaic law will be held actually more accountable: "For
not the hearers of the law are just before God, but the
doers of the law shall be justified."  (V. 13.)

Paul here is not stating the way and power by which a
man can obey law and can be just before God.  He is
simply declaring that God is impartial and will judge every
man according to his works and his light; but it is the very
design of Paul to show that on these principles no flesh can
be justified (ch. 3:20).

This question, however, arises: If only "doers of the
law" are "justified," how can the rule apply to Gentiles
who have never heard the law?  The answer is that the
general rule does apply in principle to Gentiles, for their
moral instincts and their consciences are to them what

the revealed law of Sinai is to the Jews. That they have some standards of right and wrong written, not on tablets of stone, but on their hearts, is evidenced by their actions, by their recognition of the voice of conscience, and by their expressions of moral judgments. (Vs. 14-15.)

It is evident, then, that in spite of his severe arraignment of the heathen world in the preceding chapter, Paul recognized certain indestructible moral elements as still remaining. Something good could be found in the nature of even the most degraded heathen. Some law is still written on their hearts. This is a great source of encouragement as one seeks to find an entrance into their hearts for the gospel of Christ. None is wholly indifferent to kindness and love.

It should further be noticed that Paul indicates here that conscience is universal and infallible. Of course it cannot tell a man what is right and wrong, but it never fails to indicate to him whether his purpose was consciously right or wrong. That is to say, conscience may need enlightenment but it never fails to approve or rebuke what is right or wrong in moral intention. However, for its enlightenment it needs both the revealed law of God and his glorious gospel of grace.

While recognizing that the heathen perform many deeds which accord with the requirements of law, Paul declares that they so habitually transgress this law that, judging by its requirements, they will stand condemned "in the day when God shall judge the secrets of men" (v. 16). It is further declared that all which has been said as to the certainty and the principles of divine judgment is "according to" the gospel which Paul has preached. They are essential parts of it. The good news of salvation is incomplete unless it warns men of the "wrath to come" and points out to men the need as well as the way of salvation.

Last of all, Paul declares that this divine judgment is to be administered by Jesus Christ. He is "to be the Judge of the living and the dead." Yet the burden of this very epistle is to show how he can secure pardon and purity and peace and eternal blessedness for all, whether Jews or Gentiles, who put their trust in him.

## c. The Guilt of the Jew   Chs. 2:17 to 3:8

*17 But if thou bearest the name of a Jew, and restest upon the law, and gloriest in God, 18 and knowest his will, and approvest the things that are excellent, being instructed out of the law, 19 and art confident that thou thyself art a guide of the blind, a light of them that are in darkness, 20 a corrector of the foolish, a teacher of babes, having in the law the form of knowledge and of the truth; 21 thou therefore that teachest another, teachest thou not thyself? thou that preachest a man should not steal, dost thou steal? 22 thou that sayest a man should not commit adultery, dost thou commit adultery? thou that abhorrest idols, dost thou rob temples? 23 thou who gloriest in the law, through thy transgression of the law dishonorest thou God? 24 For the name of God is blasphemed among the Gentiles because of you, even as it is written. 25 For circumcision indeed profiteth, if thou be a doer of the law: but if thou be a transgressor of the law, thy circumcision is become uncircumcision. 26 If therefore the uncircumcision keep the ordinances of the law, shall not his uncircumcision be reckoned for circumcision? 27 and shall not the uncircumcision which is by nature, if it fulfil the law, judge thee, who with the letter and circumcision art a transgressor of the law? 28 For he is not a Jew who is one outwardly; neither is that circumcision which is outward in the flesh: 29 but he is a Jew who is one inwardly; and circumcision is that of the heart, in the spirit not in the letter; whose praise is not of men, but of God.*

*1 What advantage then hath the Jew? or what is the profit of circumcision? 2 Much every way: first of all, that they were intrusted with the oracles of God. 3 For what if some were without faith? shall their want of faith make of none effect the faithfulness of God? 4 God forbid: yea, let God be found true, but every man a liar; as it is written,*

*That thou mightest be justified in thy words,*

*And mightest prevail when thou comest into judgment.*

*5 But if our unrighteousness commendeth the righteousness of God, what shall we say? Is God unrighteous who vis-iteth with wrath? (I speak after the manner of men.) 6 God forbid: for then how shall God judge the world? 7 But if the truth of God through my lie abounded unto his glory, why am I also still judged as a sinner? 8 and why not (as we are slanderously reported, and as some affirm that we say), Let us do evil, that good may come? whose condemnation is just.*

It is surprising to see how seldom men realize the rather obvious truth that great opportunities are inseparable from great obligations. This is true of those who enjoy special privileges of power or of wealth or of knowledge. One of the most striking instances is in the case of the teachers who boast infallible accuracy in their interpretation of Christian truth and yet show no more Christian love and honesty and helpfulness than the very men they denounce as heretical and false.

This was exactly the case of the Jews whom Paul is here describing. They were actually less sinful and de-graded than the Gentiles yet, judged by their conduct, and in view of their superior moral enlightenment and religious privileges, they were relatively no better; they were equally guilty in the sight of the law, and just as truly in need of the righteousness which God demands, which can be found only by faith in Christ.

(1) The superior position and responsibility of the Jew (vs. 17-20) are set forth, first, in terms defining his unique relation to God. The very name of "Jew," which he boasted, indicated that he belonged to the chosen race, the covenant people of God. The law upon which he re-lied as a guarantee of his salvation, the whole Mosaic sys-tem, and the Jews' entire civil and religious polity, were gifts from the hand of God. This very God in whom they placed a false confidence, supposing themselves the ex-clusive objects of his love even when disobeying his law, is indeed the living and true God. They did possess a

peculiar knowledge of his will, although they regarded this knowledge as itself so precious as to make corresponding obedience relatively unimportant. They claimed a unique ability to detect the most delicate shades of moral distinction, being "instructed out of the law," trained by oral instruction in the whole content of the Scriptures which are indeed the very Word of God.

The superior position of the Jew is set forth, in the second place, by four current and highly colored titles defining the Jew's relation to the heathen, which, in view of the Jew's moral failure, Paul mentions with a slight touch of ridicule: "Thou thyself art a guide of the blind, a light of them that are in darkness, a corrector of the foolish, a teacher of babes, having in the law the form [the exact outline, the precise formula] of knowledge and of the truth."

All these advantages of the Jew were real, and all these by easy comparison can be applied to Christians. They, too, have a unique relation to God as a people chosen for "his own possession"; they, too, are expected to be the moral guides and the religious leaders of the world; and if they fail to show superior virtue and unselfishness and purity and love, their guilt is correspondingly greater.

(2) The guilt of the Jew (vs. 21-24) is set forth in striking contrast with his advantages which Paul has just enumerated. He is charged with theft and adultery and sacrilege, and with other transgressions of the very law in which he gloried, by which transgression God was dishonored, and, as a result, his name was "blasphemed among the Gentiles." The last words are quoted from the Old Testament prophets, not so much as a fulfilled prophecy as a fitting descriptive phrase. In ancient days the Gentiles beheld the misery of Israel and blasphemed God as one who was not able to protect his own people and worshipers; in the time of Paul, the Gentiles were blaspheming the name of God as One who could not keep from sin his chosen people, the custodians of his law and

the special objects of his grace.

So today reproach is often brought upon the name of Christ by the inconsistencies of Christians. They are not worse than other men; they are usually much better, but in comparison with their high claims and in view of their exalted privileges, their conduct is often unworthy of their Lord. When, for instance, the world remembers the loving spirit of the Master and beholds the bitterness and unkindness of his followers, it often utters with irony the once beautiful phrase of Tertullian: "See how these Christians love one another."

(3) In the third place, to establish the guilt of the Jew, Paul answers certain objections that the Jew is supposed to make to the charge that he, as truly as the Gentile, is under the condemnation of God. (Chs. 2:25 to 3:8.)

One objection is that circumcision is of no profit or avail if those thus sealed as the people of God are nonetheless under his disapproval and wrath. To this Paul replies that a mere outward seal or sign has no validity unless it is accompanied by the faith and obedience which the sign is supposed to signify. There were, indeed, real blessings belonging to the people of God, but these were conditional upon obedience to his law. True "circumcision" was the putting away from the heart of all evil desires and thoughts. Those were God's true people, whether Jews or Gentiles, who put their trust in him and obeyed his holy will: "For he is not a Jew who is one outwardly; . . . but he is a Jew who is one inwardly."

Nor have these words of Paul lost their meaning for the Christian church. Its sacraments have deep significance when they are accompanied by faith and love, and when they express a real spiritual relation to God; but if these are absent, then church membership or sacraments or ritual observances become meaningless and empty forms. The true Christian is not a man who has merely submitted to certain rites, but one who has adopted these rites because he believes that they were established by his Lord and desires thus to express his love and devotion to him, seeking for praise "not of men, but of God." (Ch. 2:25-29.)

To Paul's charge of guilt against the Jew, another objection is supposed to be raised: Paul has proved too much; if the Jew, in spite of his possession of the law, in spite of his being sealed as a member of a chosen race, is under "the wrath of God," and is as truly under condemnation as the Gentile, then the Jew has no advantage over the Gentile, a suggestion as abhorrent to the Jew as it was contrary to his sacred Scriptures. "What advantage then hath the Jew? or what is the profit of circumcision?" (Ch. 3:1.) "Much every way," replies the apostle, "first of all, that they were intrusted with the oracles of God." (V. 2.) This trust was indeed a treasure; it did place the Jew in a position of privilege, not only because it gave to him a matchless revelation of God's will, but because it contained God's promises of a coming Savior and God's assurances that Israel should someday be a source of blessing to the whole world. The rejection of the Messiah, the unbelief of some Jews, could not "make of none effect the faithfulness of God." Rather, his punishment of those who refused to believe, and his future fulfillment of his promises of blessing, would bring into fuller light his justice and his grace.

David appreciated this principle. When he had fallen into sin, and had turned to God in penitence, he felt that his very sin was designed to bring into stronger relief the justice of God. Speaking of that justice as though it could be brought to trial, he declares its absolute and complete acquittal:

"That thou mightest be justified in thy words,
And mightest prevail when thou comest into judgment."
(V. 4.)

To this conclusion an objection is at once supposed: If the unbelief and sin of the Jew has been the occasion for the clearer revelation of the justice of God, has it not been of real service to God, and can God, will God, punish one who has thus really conferred a favor upon God?

To this objection Paul makes two solemn answers: First, on this ground there could be no judgment, for at last, every man could say that his sin had been the occasion of revealing the justice of God in punishing sin.   Second, if the good which God brings out of evil justifies the evil, then all might act on the false principle of doing evil that good might come.   However, Paul at once repudiates this principle as odious, as he turns from the denial of a future judgment as absurd.   (Vs. 5-8.)

Here Paul has brought his readers into the sphere of great mysteries, but he states clearly certain supremely important truths.

(1) God does give to some men peculiar advantages and privileges; but he requires of them proportionate faithfulness and service.   Christians do have advantages over pagans; the possession of the Bible and the gospel and the means of grace are great privileges; but judged by their conduct, in view of such advantages, Christians can make no claim of righteousness or of merit; their only hope is in the redemption that is in Jesus Christ our Lord.

(2) The promises of God to Israel are certain to be fulfilled, in spite of partial blindness and temporary unbelief.   As Paul shows more perfectly in the ninth, tenth, and eleventh chapters of the epistle, a converted Israel is yet to be a source of blessing to all the nations of the world.

(3) A coming judgment, when rewards and penalties will be determined according to conduct and opportunity, is so certain that Paul does not even pause to debate its reality.   He at once dismisses a statement which calls in question this undoubted fact.

(4) In spite of the truth that God can bring good out of evil, this result never relieves of guilt the one by whom the evil has been done.   The end never justifies the means. If an act, out of which some good comes, is not to be re-

garded as bad and is not to be punished, then any crime might be encouraged for the sake of a good result, and all real distinction between right and wrong would be obliterated. Even Paul's statement of free grace was so "slanderously reported" as to indicate that it encouraged men to sin in order that grace might abound; but here, as ever, Paul repudiated the charge. Of one who would say, "Let us do evil, that good may come," Paul declares that his "condemnation is just."

### d. The Whole World Condemned   Ch. 3:9-20

9 What then? are we better than they? No, in no wise: for we before laid to the charge both of Jews and Greeks, that they are all under sin; 10 as it is written,
There is none righteous, no, not one;
11 There is none that understandeth,
There is none that seeketh after God;
12 They have all turned aside, they are together become unprofitable;
There is none that doeth good, no, not so much as one:
13 Their throat is an open sepulchre;
With their tongues they have used deceit:
The poison of asps is under their lips:
14 Whose mouth is full of cursing and bitterness:
15 Their feet are swift to shed blood;
16 Destruction and misery are in their ways;
17 And the way of peace have they not known:
18 There is no fear of God before their eyes.
19 Now we know that what things soever the law saith, it speaketh to them that are under the law; that every mouth may be stopped, and all the world may be brought under the judgment of God: 20 because by the works of the law shall no flesh be justified in his sight; for through the law cometh the knowledge of sin.

Here Paul reaches the first great conclusion of his epistle. The Gentile has sinned against the light of nature and conscience, the Jew in defiance of revealed law; therefore the whole world is under condemnation. This conclusion is so stated as to form likewise a climax to the charge against the Jew which Paul has just been making; for it is phrased in quotations found in the Jewish Scriptures, from which Paul assumes that there can be no appeal.

The passage falls into three parts. The first states the conclusion that all are under sin. (V. 9.) The second enumerates the grounds of this judgment. (Vs. 10-18.) The third pronounces the sentence of universal condemnation. (Vs. 19-20.)

"What then?" asks the apostle, in view of peculiar privileges, "are we better than they?" Are we morally superior? Are we more acceptable to God? "No, in no wise: for we before laid to the charge both of Jews and Greeks, that they are all under sin."

The Jew may have had certain outward advantages, but morally, as Paul now definitely affirms, Jews and Greeks are on the same level; all are under the guilt and power of sin. It is true that however men may differ among themselves as to individual character, as to outward circumstances, social or religious, when they appear at the bar of God, all are on equality, all are sinners, and as such, are deserving of punishment.

The Scripture proof that all men are under sin and therefore are in need of the righteousness of God is presented in a picture Paul forms by grouping together pencil strokes made by the hands of various psalmists and prophets. It is an appalling picture of the human heart and of human weakness and sin, all the more terrible because true of even the most privileged people of God.

These quotations show first the character of sinful men (vs. 10-12), then their conduct in speech and action (vs. 15-17), and lastly the cause or source of their sin, namely, that "there is no fear of God before their eyes" (v. 18).

First, then, as to the general state of mankind as under sin, Paul insists negatively that "there is none righteous, no, not one." This total lack of righteousness is traced to the fact of an entire absence of moral intelligence: "There is none that understandeth." With no real knowledge of

God and of related duties it is impossible for one to be righteous. Then, further, "there is none that seeketh after God." That is, there is no right affection, no desire or determination to worship God or to obey his will.

As a result, viewed in its positive aspects, there is a general apostasy from truth and virtue: "They have all turned aside"; the demoralization and degradation are complete: "They are together become unprofitable," that is to say, corrupt, useless, worthless.

As a practical result, there is a total absence of goodness. It is so universal as to admit of not a solitary exception: "There is none that doeth good, no, not so much as one."

The evil conduct of men is defined in the matter both of speech and of action. Paul mentions the throat, the tongue, the lips, the mouth. He declares, "Their throat is an open sepulchre"; that is, their throat threatens destruction. It is death to someone whenever the mouth is opened. "With their tongues they have used deceit"; that is, habitually and continually by flattering and smooth speaking they deceive and betray. "The poison of asps is under their lips"; that is, the falsehood and calumny which evil lips give out is like the poison of an adder. "Whose mouth is full of cursing and bitterness."

This last expression, indicating violent speech, forms a fit introduction to Paul's mention of conduct which is characterized by murder and oppression and fierce discord.

> "Their feet are swift to shed blood;
> Destruction and misery are in their ways;
> And the way of peace have they not known."
>> (Vs. 15-17.)

The source of all this iniquity is traced by the apostle to the absence of all true piety, to the lack of reverence and respect for God: "There is no fear of God before their eyes."

In pronouncing the sentence of God upon such sinners, Paul answers first an imaginary objection made by the

Jew to the contents of the last paragraph. He is supposed to say that the foregoing descriptions may apply to the heathen, but they cannot refer to Israel. Paul at once shows the absurdity of such a suggestion: "Now we know that what things soever the law saith, it speaketh to them that are under the law." That is, as Paul insists, the persons to whom most obviously the Old Testament Scriptures must apply are the very persons for whom and by whom these Scriptures were written. They had a twofold design: First, to silence any who might endeavor to declare their innocence; and second, that the whole human race should be placed in a position of owing to God the penalty of transgression, "that every mouth may be stopped, and all the world may be brought under the judgment of God." This is "because by the works of the law shall no flesh be justified in his sight."

Such in its essence is the great conclusion toward which Paul has been moving through all the previous chapters. He wishes to show the universal need of a righteousness which God alone can provide, and to do so he shows that law in itself is not a means whereby a man can be made just. The law has a different function: "Through the law cometh the knowledge of sin." This is its true function. It was never designed to save men or to deliver them from the power of evil. Its purpose has ever been to reveal the actual sinfulness of men. It may have other purposes; it does indeed fulfill other offices; but it is utterly powerless to meet the needs of a lost world, or to deliver men from the slavery and the guilt of sin. Whether this law is contained in the Scriptures or whether it is written on the hearts of men, "by the works of the law shall no flesh be justified."

## 2. THE DIVINE METHOD AND PROVISION
### Ch. 3:21-31

*21 But now apart from the law a righteousness of God hath been manifested, being witnessed by the law and the prophets; 22 even the righteousness of God through faith in Jesus Christ unto all them that believe; for there is no distinction; 23 for all have sinned, and fall short of the glory of God; 24 being justified freely by his grace through the redemption that is in Christ Jesus: 25 whom God set forth to be a propitiation, through faith, in his blood, to show his righteousness because of the passing over of the sins done aforetime, in the forbearance of God; 26 for the showing, I say, of his righteousness at this present season: that he might himself be just, and the justifier of him that hath faith in Jesus. 27 Where then is the glorying? It is excluded. By what manner of law? of works? Nay: but by a law of faith. 28 We reckon therefore that a man is justified by faith apart from the works of the law. 29 Or is God the God of Jews only? is he not the God of Gentiles also? Yea, of Gentiles also: 30 if so be that God is one, and he shall justify the circumcision by faith, and the uncircumcision through faith.*

*31 Do we then make the law of none effect through faith? God forbid: nay, we establish the law.*

How can a man be right with God? How can one who is guilty of sin be forgiven, pardoned, declared righteous, and regarded as though his sins had never been committed? No more important question possibly could be asked, and in all the Bible probably there is no more complete and satisfying answer than in these words of Paul. He has recorded here the very essence of the gospel which he desired to preach at Rome, the very sum and substance of the good news which this epistle sets forth.

One who wishes to know the very heart of the Christian message need ponder only these words; and one who reads them in the light of the Old Testament and the New cannot fail to be moved by their unique expression of the grace of God in Christ Jesus.

Paul has been insisting that the whole world is in need of righteousness and is under the condemnation of God; here he declares that through the atoning work of Christ a righteousness has been provided, and is offered freely to all on the ground of faith alone. This righteousness is "manifest" in the gospel. It is "apart from the law"; it is not secured by obeying the law; it is offered to those by whom the law has been broken; it is nothing which can be merited, earned, or deserved. However, it is in perfect accordance with the law, it is "witnessed by the law and the prophets," as Paul demonstrates clearly in the next chapter of this epistle. It is provided by God himself, for the "righteousness of God" (v. 22) here denotes not the attribute of divine justice but the righteousness which God offers to man.

It is received by faith. In fact, faith is its distinguishing feature; it is not a righteousness by works but a righteousness "through faith in Jesus Christ," and it is "unto all them that believe." Faith, however, is not a ground of merit, but merely the instrument by which this righteousness is received.

This righteousness of God is of universal application, as it is needed by all, "for all have sinned, and fall short of the glory of God." Paul does not mean that all have sinned equally, but all, without exception, have failed to attain the "glory," the praise, the approbation of God, and are therefore under his condemnation. All such, however, if they put their trust in Christ are "declared to be just," for here the word "justified" (v. 24) does not mean "made righteous," but declared righteous. Paul is here describing "justification"; sanctification will of course follow. Faith is certain to issue in a life of holiness. However, at once, before such a life has been lived, one who accepts Christ as a Savior is declared to be righteous.

This is due to no merit on the part of man. The source of this "justification" is the unmerited favor of God. Men are "justified freely by his grace."

However, this gracious justifying act on the part of God is not due to any indifference to sin, nor to his failure to observe moral distinctions. God has made it possible at infinite cost. It is "through the redemption that is in

Christ Jesus." This redemption, this deliverance from the guilt and power and penalty of sin was accomplished by the atoning death of Christ, "whom God set forth to be a propitiation, through faith, in his blood." This propitiatory death of Christ, however, was not intended to induce God to love sinners: "God so loved the world, that he gave his only begotten Son." In this propitiatory sacrifice God revealed his own attitude toward sin and made it possible for him to forgive sinners.

The mystery of atonement Paul does not attempt to solve. He does not explain just how the death of Christ constitutes him a "propitiation." The fact, however, is at the very heart of the Christian gospel, and Paul does make it clear that the supreme element in propitiation is the vindicating of divine righteousness: "To show his righteousness because of the passing over of the sins done aforetime, in the forbearance of God." (V. 25.) Here the phrase "righteousness of God" denotes his attribute of justice. It was necessary for him to show his unchanging attitude toward sin. During past generations God appeared to deal lightly with transgressors; he seemed almost indifferent to their guilt. Occasionally he gave some signal manifestation of divine displeasure and inflicted some startling penalty, but he was long-suffering and gracious and allowed men living in sin to attain old age; even whole nations were permitted to continue for long periods openly violating his sacred laws. However, in the death of his own Son, God made it evident once and for all that he is not indifferent to sin. The cross is the vindication of his righteousness. However, it is much more. It is the means of salvation for man; for it is in view of the cross that God now, "at this present season," can "himself be just, and the justifier of him that hath faith in Jesus." One who accepts the crucified Savior as his Lord really submits to the divine sentence upon sin; he becomes right with God. He is declared to be just; and God who thus justifies sinners is shown to be just.

There are mysteries involved, but there is no doubt that as one gazes upon the cross of Christ, he feels the burden of guilt roll away, and he finds peace with God and power for a new and higher life.

Paul has completed his superb statement of the great principle of justification by faith; however, as the chapter closes (vs. 27-31), he adds certain inferences by which the principle is commended and established.

First, boasting is excluded. "A law," or divine ordinance, or spiritual institution, whereby a man rests for his salvation wholly upon the merits and work of Christ, must make it impossible for such a man to glory or to boast in the presence of God. Therefore, Paul concludes, "a man is justified by faith apart from the works of the law"; his justification is entirely aside from any obedience to the law; it is by faith alone. As Paul elsewhere shows, faith will result in obedience, and justification will issue in holy living, but the truth that justification is by faith alone is the very heart of Christianity. It is rightly regarded as "the article of a standing or falling church."

Secondly, by this "law" of justification, God is presented in his true character. If some men are saved by a law of works and some by a law of faith, then there must be two Gods, an idea absolutely abhorrent to the Jew. However, since there is but one God, "the God of Jews," who is "the God of Gentiles also," therefore, there can be but one way of salvation, and the only possible method of justification must be by faith in Christ.

Last of all, Paul raises the imaginary objection that justification by faith makes "the law of none effect." It is said to obliterate all moral distinctions, to regard law as useless and worthless, to annul the divine ordinances recorded in the Old Testament Scriptures. On the contrary, Paul states, by declaring this doctrine "we establish the law." He demonstrates this claim in various parts of the epistle, and first of all in the chapter which immediately follows.

### 3. THE PROOF FROM SCRIPTURE   Ch. 4

*1 What then shall we say that Abraham, our forefather, hath found according to the flesh? 2 For if Abraham was justified by works, he hath whereof to glory; but not toward God. 3 For what saith the scripture? And Abraham believed God, and it was reckoned unto him for righteousness. 4 Now to him that worketh, the reward is not reckoned as of grace, but as of debt. 5 But to him that worketh not, but believeth on him that justifieth the ungodly, his faith is reckoned for righteousness. 6 Even as David also pronounceth blessing upon the man, unto whom God reckoneth righteousness apart from works, 7* saying,*

Blessed are they whose iniquities are forgiven,
And whose sins are covered.*

*8     Blessed is the man to whom the Lord will not reckon
sin.*

*9 Is this blessing then pronounced upon the circumcision, or upon the uncircumcision also? for we say, To Abraham his faith was reckoned for righteousness. 10 How then was it reckoned? when he was in circumcision, or in uncircumcision? Not in circumcision, but in uncircumcision: 11 and he received the sign of circumcision, a seal of the righteousness of the faith which he had while he was in uncircumcision: that he might be the father of all them that believe, though they be in uncircumcision, that righteousness might be reckoned unto them; 12 and the father of circumcision to them who not only are of the circumcision, but who also walk in the steps of that faith of our father Abraham which he had in uncircumcision. 13 For not through the law was the promise to Abraham or to his seed that he should be heir of the world, but through the righteousness of faith. 14 For if they that are of the law are heirs, faith is made void, and the promise is made of none effect: 15 for the law worketh wrath; but where there is no law, neither is there transgression. 16 For this cause* it is *of faith, that* it may be *according to grace; to the end that the promise may be sure to all the seed; not to that only which is of the law, but to that also which is of the faith of Abraham, who is the father of us all 17 (as it is written, A father of many nations have I made thee) before him*

*whom he believed, even God, who giveth life to the dead,
and calleth the things that are not, as though they were.
18 Who in hope believed against hope, to the end that he
might become a father of many nations, according to
that which had been spoken, So shall thy seed be.  19 And
without being weakened in faith he considered his own
body now as good as dead (he being about a hundred years
old), and the deadness of Sarah's womb; 20 yet, looking
unto the promise of God, he wavered not through unbelief,
but waxed strong through faith, giving glory to God, 21 and
being fully assured that what he had promised, he was able
also to perform.  22 Wherefore also it was reckoned unto
him for righteousness.  23 Now it was not written for his
sake alone, that it was reckoned unto him; 24 but for our
sake also, unto whom it shall be reckoned, who believe on
him that raised Jesus our Lord from the dead, 25 who was
delivered up for our trespasses, and was raised for our justification.*

When Paul has clearly defined the doctrine of justification by faith, he naturally turns for the confirmation of
its truth to the Old Testament. He still has in mind the
Jew who is supposed to feel that this doctrine sets aside
the inspired Scriptures.  In these Scriptures, on the contrary, Paul finds the most unanswerable evidence that his
teaching is true. He selects the crucial case of Abraham,
the father of the Jewish race, the most impressive and
important figure who appears upon the stage of human
history between Adam and Christ.

a. The case of Abraham is decisive, at least to the mind
of the Jew, because he towered above all other men in his
moral grandeur, and if anyone was accepted of God, it
must have been he, for he was known as the "friend of
God."  If he was not justified by works, no man could
be; if he was justified by faith, there can be no other way
of justification for any man.  (Vs. 1-8.)  "What then shall
we say that Abraham, our forefather, hath found according to the flesh?"  The last clause refers to the human nature which he shared with all men.  The question then is,

What did Abraham attain through his own natural efforts?
How was he justified? Was it on the ground of his illus-
trious acts? These gave him a place of honor among men,
but did they secure his justification and thus give him a
ground of boasting before God? "What saith the scripture? And Abraham believed God, and it was reckoned
unto him for righteousness." Nothing is said here about
works; it is his faith, his trust and confidence in God,
which is "reckoned," imputed, accounted unto him as
righteousness. Abraham, therefore, did not earn righteousness; he received it as a free gift. A laborer who
works for pay can claim his wages as a debt that is due;
but such was not the case with the old patriarch; and such
is never the case when a man is justified by God. It is to
one who has no confidence in his own works, but trusts in
a God who justifies freely, and actually does pronounce
righteous an ungodly man—it is to such a one that "faith is
reckoned for righteousness" (v. 5).

To this great truth David likewise testifies in the Thirty-
second Psalm when he says:

"Blessed are they whose iniquities are forgiven,
 And whose sins are covered.
 Blessed is the man to whom the Lord will not
   reckon sin."

The psalmist thus pronounces happy, not one who has
kept the law, not one who is being rewarded for his good
"works," but one who has broken the law and who, as he
has turned toward God in penitence and trust, has been
forgiven and declared to be just. Nothing could be more
clear, nothing more startling, yet nothing more comforting, than the truth that when we are conscious of our sins
and turn to God in the name of Christ, trusting in his redeeming grace, we are pardoned and justified and can
know the joy of salvation.

b. That justification is possible for all, Paul next declares when he shows how it is as independent of religious

ceremonies or of special privileges as it is of boasted deeds of the law. Justification is by faith alone, although the experience inevitably results in holy living; so too, faith naturally is expressed in religious rites; but before these, and aside from these, God justifies those who believe in Jesus. (Vs. 9-11.)

This is what Paul means by asking whether justification was granted to those alone who had received the sacramental seal of circumcision, or to all who trusted in God and accepted his promises of grace. That righteousness was independent, and preceded any such external rite, was evident from the case of Abraham, for he was justified before he received this seal.

Paul takes us back to that night when the aged patriarch, standing childless and alone under the Syrian sky, received from the Lord the promise that his seed should become as the stars of the sky in multitude. Then it was, we are told, that he "believed God, and it was reckoned unto him for righteousness." It was years after that Abraham received circumcision as a seal of the covenant promise of God. Justification, then, preceded and was quite independent of circumcision, yet the latter became "a seal of the righteousness of the faith which he had while he was in uncircumcision" (v. 11).

Therefore, Abraham became, in the spiritual realm, "the father of all them that believe," whether Jews or Gentiles, and his own experience became a proof that men are justified independently of all ceremonies and rites. The latter may be regarded as seals by which covenants are confirmed; they may be signs and symbols of benefits conferred, but in themselves they are powerless, and their efficacy is dependent upon the faith of the recipient and the grace of God the Giver. The real descendants of Abraham, therefore, are not those literal Israelites who are lineal descendants of Abraham, nor yet are they those who imitate his acceptance of ceremonial rites, but those who emulate and share his faith. To them as to him, faith is "reckoned" "for righteousness."

c. This righteousness is independent of law and is received by faith alone; in the case of Abraham, faith evidently was the acceptance of a promise and not obedience to law. It was, however, vital and unquestioning, and it accepted as certain what reason might have ridiculed or denied. (Vs. 13-22.)

The promise to Abraham, in its ultimate scope, was "that he should be heir of the world." The fulfillment of this promise was to be realized through Christ and his followers. In a true sense they yet are to "inherit the earth." Yet for Abraham this hope was not conditioned upon the fulfillment of law, but upon a righteousness which resulted from faith. (V. 13.)

"Faith" and "promise" belong to a different domain from that of "law." The latter would exclude the former, and make them of no effect. The real effect of law is to bring condemnation. Where "there is no law," there may be fault and sin, but not "transgression"; that is, no actual breach of law, which is to say that "law," instead of bringing blessing, has no power but that of increasing guilt and of making men liable to the "wrath of God." (Vs. 14-15.)

For this reason it was the plan of God to condition his great blessings not upon obedience to law but upon faith, for faith as exercised by man implies "grace" on the part of God; and such a system made the fulfillment of the promise possible, not only to those who had the Mosaic law, but to all persons who, by their faith in God, are true children of Abraham. Thus, as Christian believers, we can claim that Abraham is "the father of us all," and can share in all the blessedness promised to him when God called him "a father of many nations" (vs. 16-17).

Possibly this reasoning of Paul seems somewhat difficult to follow; but its great essential teaching is clear and is full of comfort for every reader, for it gives assurance that, through faith alone, may be received all the blessed promises of God, for eternity as well as for time.

The faith of Abraham was extraordinary in the extreme.

It was, however, centered upon God, "who giveth life to the dead, and calleth the things that are not, as though they were" (v. 17). In such a God he evidently trusted, for when he received the promise he was as good as dead and his heart no longer cherished the hope of an heir. Yet, contrary to all human probability that the promise could be fulfilled, and fully conscious of all the apparent impossibilities involved, he praised God for the miracle which was to be performed, "being fully assured that what he had promised, he was able also to perform." It was through such faith that Abraham became "a father of many nations"; it was such faith that God graciously "reckoned unto him for righteousness" (v. 22).

Such faith, indeed, was extraordinary, but its essence was quite plain. It consisted in taking God at his word, in believing that what he said was true, in trusting that what God promised he would bring to pass. Nor does our faith differ from this in kind. God does not expect us to believe what is irrational, but he promises blessings that we cannot explain, which will be granted by methods we cannot understand. We are conscious of unworthiness and fault, but he promises to pardon, cleanse, relieve; we come with simple faith in the power of Christ and find forgiveness, peace, and rest. He promises us resurrection and endless glory and by faith we die with hopes reaching beyond the grave.

d. It is indeed in the sphere of death and resurrection that the thoughts revolve all through these paragraphs, and particularly as we reach the great application of the story with which the chapter closes (vs. 23-25). All this narrative, Paul declares, "was not written for his sake alone," simply to record that Abraham was justified by faith, "but for our sake also," to assure us that we, too, receive a similar acceptance if we have a like faith. The promise to Abraham was practically that of life from the dead. As Christians we trust the same God who also "raised Jesus our Lord from the dead" and conditions our pardon and acceptance and righteousness upon our faith in him "who was delivered up for our trespasses, and was raised for our justification." The death and resurrection of Christ are inseparably united as the ground of our salvation; yet they can be distinguished in their purpose and effect. Looking at them separately, we see that Paul could here mean that Christ died to atone for our sins and rose again with a view to securing our justification. As, however, the word "for" should probably be interpreted in the same sense in both clauses, the more exact meaning may be that Christ who was surrendered to death because of the offenses we had committed, was raised to life because of the acquittal he had secured for us. Whatever the exact translation may be, it is clear that the resurrection was "the crown and seal to the atonement wrought by his death," and that it evokes the faith which makes his atoning work effectual for believers. In any case, the inspiring truth is taught that our justification is secured by the death and resurrection of our Lord, and if this is its ground, then surely in such a plan of salvation there can be no place for pride or self-reliance or human merit, but only for humble, confident, grateful faith. As the whole chapter has therefore shown, the Old Testament Scriptures agree with the New in assuring us that faith alone is the way by which men can be justified in the sight of God.

## 4. THE BLESSED RESULTS   Ch. 5:1-11

*1 Being therefore justified by faith, we have peace with God through our Lord Jesus Christ; 2 through whom also we have had our access by faith into this grace wherein we stand; and we rejoice in hope of the glory of God. 3 And not only so, but we also rejoice in our tribulations: knowing that tribulation worketh stedfastness; 4 and stedfastness, approvedness; and approvedness, hope: 5 and hope putteth not to shame; because the love of God hath been shed abroad in our hearts through the Holy Spirit which was given unto us. 6 For while we were yet weak, in due sea-*

*son Christ died for the ungodly. 7 For scarcely for a righteous man will one die: for peradventure for the good man some one would even dare to die. 8 But God commendeth his own love toward us, in that, while we were yet sinners, Christ died for us. 9 Much more then, being now justified by his blood, shall we be saved from the wrath of God through him. 10 For if, while we were enemies, we were reconciled to God through the death of his Son, much more, being reconciled, shall we be saved by his life; 11 and not only so, but we also rejoice in God through our Lord Jesus Christ, through whom we have now received the reconciliation.*

Paul has already exhibited the need, the exact nature, and the Scriptural proof of the doctrine of "justification by faith." He now presents some of its blessed consequences. It is true that practically the whole remaining portion of the epistle unfolds the new life of holiness and happiness which issues from justification. Here, however, the stress is laid upon the acceptance with God which the justified enjoy, and upon their certainty of sharing his eternal glory. In fact, this certainty of salvation is the essential burden of this passage (vs. 1-11). The questions might naturally arise as to whether the trials and tribulations incident to the life of a Christian may not cause faith to fail, and whether believers may not be swept away from their position of acceptance with God. Paul here gives the assurance that justification by faith is permanent and is sure to issue in blessedness which is eternal.

a. First of all, then, is the assurance that "being therefore justified by faith, we have peace with God through our Lord Jesus Christ." When Paul speaks here of "peace with God," his phrase is not equivalent to "peace from God," or to "the peace of God." The latter may denote the peace which God himself enjoys, or the peace which he inspires in the hearts of his children. But "peace with God" denotes a relation to him. It indicates pardon and acceptance and is contrasted with enmity or wrath. It

signifies the position of those who once were under condemnation but now are enjoying the full measure of divine
forgiveness and favor. It is a relation with God which
results from the atoning work of Christ, and in consequence of this relation a peace which is not born of earth
enters the souls of the justified, a peace which God sup-
plies, a peace in some measure like to that which the "God
of peace" himself enjoys.

b. It is through Christ also that "we have had our access by faith into this grace wherein we stand." As our
peace with God is grounded on the atoning death of Christ,
so it is by the power of the living Christ that we are
brought into the atmosphere and position of conscious
peace and acceptance with God. "This grace wherein we
stand" is more fully described in the eighth chapter of this
same epistle; and there it is pictured as the position of
sons who live in fellowship with God, who are not merely
forgiven enemies or pardoned sinners, but children who
have received "the spirit of adoption" whereby they cry
"Abba, Father." It is Christ who has given us such "access" to God, such an "introduction" as persons of note
are given into the presence chamber of a king. Only
those who are conscious of being justified can really enjoy that true fellowship with God which is made possible
by Jesus Christ our Lord.

c. It is, however, not peace with Christ, nor the position of sons, but the prospect of glory which forms the
chief element of that blessedness of justified souls here set
forth: "We rejoice in hope of the glory of God" (v. 2). As
Paul argues more fully in the eighth chapter of the epistle,
"If children, then heirs; heirs of God, and joint-heirs with
Christ; if so be that we suffer with him, that we may be
also glorified with him." To share such heavenly splendor, to behold the King in his beauty, to be like him when
we see him as he is, all this is the inspiring hope of those
who have been justified by faith in Christ. Nor is this
hope dimmed—it rather is brightened—by the distress and

trials which now encompass us. The secret lies in the purpose and results of these very persecutions and trials, so that "we also rejoice in our tribulations," knowing that these tribulations result in steadfastness, in approvedness, or tried integrity, and this in turn issues in a stronger and clearer hope. Thus the very tribulations become a ground and a source of strength for that confident expectation of glory which belongs to the justified.

And this "hope putteth not to shame," it does not deceive, it does not mock us, it is not disappointed, and for two reasons. First, "because the love of God hath been shed abroad in our hearts through the Holy Spirit which was given unto us." This is the first mention in the letter of the Spirit; in the eighth chapter are found some of the most significant statements in reference to his work which the Bible contains. This first mention reminds us that his power and influence make us conscious and certain of the love which God has toward us.

There is, however, a ground of hope outside ourselves, and this is found in a historic fact, in that supreme fact, namely, the atoning death of Christ: "For while we were yet weak, in due season Christ died for the ungodly" (v. 6). Sin is here called weakness. As sinners we are pictured as suffering from moral infirmity and as in need of healing and of strength. It was for us that Christ died "in due season," or, as Paul says elsewhere, "when the fulness of the time came," to meet the great crisis which sin had produced.

Here Paul states that "Christ died for the ungodly." We had expected him to say that he died for us, but the substitution of this word brings out all the more clearly the thought of the great love of God in sending his Son to die for the undeserving. This is emphasized in the verses which follow, where, in contrast with the love of man for man, we have the demonstration of the love of God toward us. Paul intimates that while it might be possible that one would not die for a righteous man, yet for a "good man," a loving, a deserving man, "some one would even dare to die." This possible manifestation of human love, however, is far surpassed by the love of God who "commendeth his own love toward us, in that, while we were yet sinners, Christ died for us."

The argument which Paul advances is this: If God so loved us while we were yet sinners, "much more then, being now justified by his blood, shall we be saved from the wrath of God through him." If God has done so much for his enemies, what will he not do for his friends? "For if, while we were enemies, we were reconciled to God through the death of his Son, much more, being reconciled, shall we be saved by his life." It is evident that our eternal salvation is secure and certain. The God who made possible for us justification through the death of his Son, will undoubtedly grant us eternal blessedness as we share now in the life of the risen Christ.

No wonder, then, that Paul closes the paragraph with the assurance that we who are justified have triumphant joy in God through our Lord Jesus Christ, through whom we have now received reconciliation. Such peace with God, such access to a loving Father, such unclouded hope of glory, are the sure and inevitable blessings of all who are justified by faith.

### 5. THE UNIVERSAL APPLICATION   Ch. 5:12-21

*12 Therefore, as through one man sin entered into the world, and death through sin; and so death passed unto all men, for that all sinned:—13 for until the law sin was in the world; but sin is not imputed when there is no law. 14 Nevertheless death reigned from Adam until Moses, even over them that had not sinned after the likeness of Adam's transgression, who is a figure of him that was to come. 15 But not as the trespass, so also is the free gift. For if by the trespass of the one the many died, much more did the grace of God, and the gift by the grace of the one man, Jesus Christ, abound unto the many. 16 And not as*

*through one that sinned,* so *is the gift: for the judgment*
came *of one unto condemnation, but the free gift* came *of
many trespasses unto justification. 17 For if, by the trespass of the one, death reigned through the one; much more
shall they that receive the abundance of grace and of the
gift of righteousness reign in life through the one,* even
*Jesus Christ. 18 So then as through one trespass* the judgment came *unto all men to condemnation; even so through
one act of righteousness* the free gift came *unto all men to
justification of life. 19 For as through the one man's disobedience the many were made sinners, even so through
the obedience of the one shall the many be made righteous.
20 And the law came in besides, that the trespass might
abound; but where sin abounded, grace did abound more
exceedingly: 21 that, as sin reigned in death, even so might
grace reign through righteousness unto eternal life through
Jesus Christ our Lord.*

The analogy drawn by Paul between Adam and Christ
is judged to be one of the most difficult and complex passages of the epistle. By some readers it is regarded as a
parenthesis or break in the argument. By others, however, probably more correctly, it is looked upon as a climax to the discussion of the doctrine of justification by
faith and as an introduction to the treatment of the doctrine of sanctification, or of the life of holiness in which
justification issues.

It does, indeed, confirm the doctrine of justification by
faith by showing that the same principles of divine government are involved in justifying those who are united to
Christ by faith as in condemning those who share the nature and sin of Adam. On the other hand, by advancing
from the truth of justification by faith in Christ to that of
vital union with Christ, the ground is laid for the teaching
which follows as to the sanctification and final glory of
believers. (Chs. 6 to 8.)

Possibly the most important relation which this famous
analogy sustains to the foregoing argument is in showing
the wide application of justification; as the paragraph im-

mediately preceding reveals its permanence (vs. 1-11), this paragraph declares its universality (vs. 12-21). The sum of the message is simply this: As the sin of Adam brought sin and death to all mankind, so the redeeming work of Christ brings righteousness and life to all who are united to him by a living faith.

The analogy involves not only such a comparison (vs. 12, 18, 19) but also certain contrasts (vs. 15, 16, 17). The comparison begins with a statement of the universal reign of sin and death due to the sin of Adam: "Therefore, as through one man sin entered into the world, and death through sin; and so death passed unto all men, for that all sinned." The specific sin to which Paul here refers is unquestionably that act of disobedience on the part of Adam commonly designated as "the fall," and believed to be, as here intimated, the source of all human sinfulness and misery and death. By the last term, Paul evidently meant physical death, although it indicates all the misery and distress of which the death of the body is the symbol, including ultimately that separation from God which is the final penalty of sin. The penalty, Paul declares, has been visited on the whole human race in virtue of the fact "that all sinned." This last statement is commonly interpreted to mean that the guilt of Adam has been imputed to his descendants. It more probably refers to the actual guilt which men incur because of that tendency to evil which they inherit, which is believed to be a result of the disobedience of Adam. It is probably to be interpreted as a simple statement of the universal prevalence of sin, and of death which is its penalty, in order that Paul may compare with it the wide influence of the saving work of Christ.

Before completing this comparison, Paul pauses to demonstrate the fact that sin is universal. He does so by stating that "until the law sin was in the world." This sin, however, was not in the nature of actual disobedience to a command as in the case of Adam, or of his descendants who received the law of Moses. Nevertheless, between Adam and Moses there was real sin; because death reigned like a cruel tyrant, all were subject to his power. There must, therefore, have been disobedience to law, not the law of Moses but the law written on the human heart. This universal sin could be traced as an effect "of Adam's transgression, who is a figure of him that was to come." This universal result of Adam's sin is about to be compared with the salvation accomplished by Christ, but Paul first pauses to mention three contrasts between the work of the first and of the last Adam. There is a contrast in quality: the one is all of sin, the other of bounty and of grace. "But not as the trespass, so also is the free gift. For if by the trespass of the one the many died, much more did the grace of God, and the gift by the grace of the one man, Jesus Christ, abound unto the many."

So, too, there is a contrast in the quantity or the mode of working. In the case of Adam, the sentence pronounced was due to the act of a single man and had as its result a sweeping verdict of condemnation; but in the case of Christ, his work had its rise in many faults and its result in a declaration of pardon and righteousness: "And not as through one that sinned, so is the gift: for the judgment came of one unto condemnation, but the free gift came of many trespasses unto justification."

There was a third contrast: there was a difference in the whole character and consequence of the work of Adam and of Christ. Through the fault of one man, death, through that sole agency, began to reign as a cruel tyrant. On the other hand, those who receive the gift of righteousness shall reign in life through the power of Christ, "For if, by the trespass of the one, death reigned through the one; much more shall they that receive the abundance of grace and of the gift of righteousness reign in life through the one, even Jesus Christ."

When at last Paul comes to complete his great comparison and to show that the wide effect of the sin of Adam has its parallel in the universal benefit accruing to all who put their trust in Christ, he does so by showing that as one act of disobedience resulted in bringing all men under condemnation, so "one act of righteousness," namely, the voluntary death of Christ for the sins of the world, brings justification to all who put their trust in him. "So then as through one trespass the judgment came unto all men to condemnation; even so through one act of righteousness the free gift came unto all men to justification of life." Then, to sum up his entire analogy, Paul concludes, "For as through the one man's disobedience the many were made sinners, even so through the obedience of the one shall the many be made righteous."

It remains only for the apostle to show the true function of the law. He has stated that, even between Adam and Moses, sin and death had reigned supreme. In the earlier portion of his epistle he has shown that the law was unable to secure justification for men. What, then, was its province? Paul here declares that it "came in besides, that the trespass might abound." Instead of relieving men from the guilt of sin, it actually led to the multiplication of sins. But through the work of Christ a glorious result was achieved: "Where sin abounded, grace did abound more exceedingly." Until the coming of Christ, sin ruled in the realm of death like a pitiless monarch; but since the redeeming work of our Lord, grace has been enthroned and given sway over the followers of Christ, so that they may be delivered from death and made heirs of eternal life (vs. 20-21). Thus Paul not only shows the wide application of the justifying grace of God but also indicates what in the next chapter he proceeds to develop, namely, that its issue is life in its largest and truest aspects, both for time and for eternity.

This is one of the most intricate and perplexing paragraphs in the Bible, and therefore its interpretation demands both humility and charity. Unfortunately, it has been for centuries the battlefield of theological controversy.

Its statements are so profound and its implications are so wide that all readers should not expect to agree upon their meaning. The main message, however, is clear. It is intended to show the gracious provision which God has made for a race which has fallen wholly under the dominance of sin and of death, a provision of righteousness and of eternal life made possible through the atoning work and divine power of Jesus Christ our Lord.

## B. THE LIFE OF THE BELIEVERS Chs. 6 to 8

### 1. DEAD TO SIN AND ALIVE UNTO GOD
### Ch. 6:1-14

1 What shall we say then? Shall we continue in sin, that grace may abound? 2 God forbid. We who died to sin, how shall we any longer live therein? 3 Or are ye ignorant that all we who were baptized into Christ Jesus were baptized into his death? 4 We were buried therefore with him through baptism into death: that like as Christ was raised from the dead through the glory of the Father, so we also might walk in newness of life. 5 For if we have become united with him in the likeness of his death, we shall be also in the likeness of his resurrection; 6 knowing this, that our old man was crucified with him, that the body of sin might be done away, that so we should no longer be in bondage to sin; 7 for he that hath died is justified from sin. 8 But if we died with Christ, we believe that we shall also live with him; 9 knowing that Christ being raised from the dead dieth no more; death no more hath dominion over him. 10 For the death that he died, he died unto sin once: but the life that he liveth, he liveth unto God. 11 Even so reckon ye also yourselves to be dead unto sin, but alive unto God in Christ Jesus.

12 Let not sin therefore reign in your mortal body, that ye should obey the lusts thereof: 13 neither present your members unto sin as instruments of unrighteousness; but present yourselves unto God, as alive from the dead, and your members as instruments of righteousness unto God. 14 For sin shall not have dominion over you: for ye are not under law, but under grace.

The doctrine of justification by faith always has been exposed to misunderstanding, misinterpretation, and abuse. Therefore, when Paul has completed his exposition of the doctrine, it is natural that he should state and answer three most familiar objections offered by its opponents. The first is that such a method of declaring men just, encourages sin (ch. 6:1-14); the second, that it allows sin (chs. 6:15 to 7:6); and the third, that it makes law a sinful or an evil thing (ch. 7:7-25).

The common fallacy in all these objections, and in most criticisms of the doctrine of justification by faith, consists in the failure to understand what is meant by faith. If faith denotes mere assent to dogmas or the repetition of a creed, then to accept one as righteous, in view of his faith, would be absurd and unjust; but faith describes a personal relation to Christ. For a believer, it means trust in Christ, obedience to Christ, love for Christ; and such trust and obedience and love inevitably result in purity and holiness and a life of unselfish service. Justification by faith cannot encourage sin, or allow sin, or discredit the law of God. It must result rather in righteousness and true obedience. Justification, therefore, issues in sanctification. The two may be separated in thought, but they are united in experience. For one who is justified by faith, there begins at the same time a new life of holiness. Of this new life Paul treats in this and the two following chapters (chs. 6 to 8).

First of all, then, Paul notices the objection that justification by faith encourages sin: "What shall we say then? Shall we continue in sin, that grace may abound?" (Ch. 6:1.) Paul has been saying that the giving of the law resulted in definite transgressions and in the increase of guilt, but that these were met by God's gracious justification, so that "where sin abounded, grace did abound more exceedingly." Shall we say, then, that such justifying grace encourages sin? If God forgives freely, and by such forgiveness magnifies his grace, shall we not sin more continually that thus his grace may abound?

Paul at once repudiates the suggestion: "God forbid."

Then he shows that such an intimation is contrary to experience and to reason: "We who died to sin, how shall we any longer live therein?" We Christians by our confession and by our faith are identified with Christ. This vital union with him is such that we experience in the moral sphere all that he experienced in the physical, when he died and was buried and rose again. If we are united with him who died for our sins, we are understood to have "died to sin." We are supposed to be blind to its enticements, to be deaf to its commands, to be insensible to its power.

Paul makes the truth more plain by a reference to Christian baptism: "Or are ye ignorant that all we who were baptized into Christ Jesus were baptized into his death? We were buried therefore with him through baptism into death: that like as Christ was raised from the dead through the glory of the Father, so we also might walk in newness of life." These figures of speech are commonly taken as referring to immersion. This mode of baptism quite possibly may have been in the apostle's mind. However, such a reference should not prove that immersion is the only valid mode of baptism. The New Testament and the practice of the early church both indicate that baptism was administered by pouring (affusion) or by sprinkling, as well as by immersion.

Nor is the mode of baptism the important feature in this reference. Paul here emphasizes not the rite or ceremony but the profession and the faith which accompany baptism, which alone give to it significance and meaning. According to this profession and in virtue of this faith, we Christians who have submitted to this rite have ended the old life of sin. As far as sin is concerned we are dead and buried, and "as Christ was raised from the dead" through the glorious power of God, so by the power of the risen Christ we should experience and should show a life of new virtue and holiness. "For if we have become united with him in the likeness of his death, we shall be also in the likeness of his resurrection." Paul further enlarges upon the idea of death to sin by reminding us that as Christians "our old man was crucified" with Christ. That is to say, our old dispositions and appetites and evil desires have been put to death. These are pictured as a "body of sin" which was put to death on the cross with Christ. Sin is described as the slave master who was in control of our former life; but since we died to sin, we are now declared to be liberated from this bondage.

The Christian life, however, is not merely negative. It does not consist simply in freedom from sin. It is a new and risen life, lived by the power of the risen Christ. Therefore, Paul declares, "If we died with Christ, we believe that we shall also live with him." As he died once for all and now lives unto God, we, too, are regarded as having died to sin once for all that henceforth and forever we may live in obedience to God. This is what the apostle means by his exhortation, "Even so reckon ye also yourselves to be dead unto sin, but alive unto God in Christ Jesus." So we are to regard ourselves. We are not to imagine, however, for a moment that in reality such a death has taken place. Our evil passions and dispositions are still active and powerful. We must, however, disown their rule. We must trust in Christ for strength. The life of a Christian need not be one merely of ceaseless conflict; it should be a life of ever more continuous victory.

This is the truth which Paul has in mind as he gives his closing exhortation. He urges us to make more real in our experience the ideal state which he has been describing. He urges us to disown the reign of sin, to refuse to obey its evil desires, not to offer our bodies as instruments of unrighteousness but, as belonging to those who have risen from the dead, to present our "members as instruments of righteousness unto God." The reason which he assigns for such an exhortation is that as believers in Christ, joined to him in a vital union, sin shall not have dominion over us, for, the apostle declares, "ye are not

under law, but under grace." Law, as Paul will proceed
to show, has in itself no power to deliver. It rather becomes an incentive to sin, and it increases guilt. Grace,
however, is sufficient for all our needs, and that method
of justification which is by faith and issues from grace results in an experience which can be truly designated as
dead to sin and alive unto God.

### 2. FREE FROM SIN AND SERVANTS OF RIGHTEOUSNESS   Ch. 6:15-23

*15 What then? shall we sin, because we are not under
law, but under grace? God forbid. 16 Know ye not, that
to whom ye present yourselves as servants unto obedience,
his servants ye are whom ye obey; whether of sin unto
death, or of obedience unto righteousness? 17 But thanks
be to God, that, whereas ye were servants of sin, ye became
obedient from the heart to that form of teaching whereunto
ye were delivered; 18 and being made free from sin, ye became servants of righteousness. 19 I speak after the manner of men because of the infirmity of your flesh: for as ye
presented your members as servants to uncleanness and to
iniquity unto iniquity, even so now present your members
as servants to righteousness unto sanctification. 20 For
when ye were servants of sin, ye were free in regard of
righteousness. 21 What fruit then had ye at that time in
the things whereof ye are now ashamed? for the end of
those things is death. 22 But now being made free from
sin and become servants to God, ye have your fruit unto
sanctification, and the end eternal life. 23 For the wages of
sin is death; but the free gift of God is eternal life in Christ
Jesus our Lord.*

Every soul must know something of the degrading, mysterious slavery of sin. It is felt to be at once a fault and
a misfortune. One voluntarily yields to the voice of evil,
and at the same time finds himself unable to refuse. Deliverance comes through faith in Christ whose service is
true freedom. Such is the message of Paul as he here

describes true Christians as free from sin and servants of righteousness.

He is answering a second supposed objection to the doctrine of justification by faith, namely, that it allows sin. The first objection was that if justification is due to the grace of God and not to the merit of man, it really encourages sin, for the greater the sin, the greater would be the manifestation of divine grace (ch. 6:1). This second objection, however, is somewhat different. It proposes the difficulty that if one is justified who has not kept the law, then one must be free to break the law. "What then? shall we sin, because we are not under law, but under grace?" (Ch. 6:15.) Paul at once indignantly rejects the suggestion. "God forbid," he exclaims, and he proceeds to show that faith in Christ does not make one free to sin, but free from sin: "Know ye not, that to whom ye present yourselves as servants unto obedience, his servants ye are whom ye obey; whether of sin unto death, or of obedience unto righteousness?" To yield obedience and service to any person is to become a slave of that person, and as no one really can serve two masters, either he is a slave of sin, a slavery resulting in death, or he is a servant of Christ, a service which results in righteousness.

Paul thanks God, however, that his readers who once were servants of sin have yielded themselves to Christ and are giving hearty obedience to that standard of life and conduct in which they were instructed as Christian converts, so that "being made free from sin" they have become "servants of righteousness" (vs. 17-18). Paul explains that in thus speaking of slavery he is using a figure of speech taken from familiar human relations, and that he employs so unpleasant a metaphor because he wishes to make plain to the defective spiritual apprehension of his readers their true relation to sin and to righteousness, and to exhort them to make real in their experience all that they profess as followers of Christ and all that is possible for them through the grace of God.

If indeed they have been justified, if their faith is real, if they truly belong to Christ, there must be no divided allegiance. As they formerly devoted themselves to the service of moral defilement and increasing lawlessness, so now they must devote the members of their bodies to the service of righteousness, so to become more and more truly consecrated to God.

Paul is the more earnest in his exhortation in view of their previous service of sin and its pitiful results in contrast with the possibilities of their present service of Christ.

When servants of sin they had been "free in regard of righteousness," not that righteousness had no claims upon them, but that they had been heedless of its demands. The results had been such as are remembered only with deepest shame, and such as could result only in death.

By way of contrast, however, Paul encourages his readers by the assurance that "now being made free from sin and become servants to God," they can put forth activities which will result in a progressive state of increasing holiness which will have its ultimate issue in eternal life. (Vs. 21-22.) Paul enforces his exhortation and his encouragement by the solemn statement and blessed assurance: "For the wages of sin is death; but the free gift of God is eternal life in Christ Jesus our Lord." Sin is still represented here as a cruel slave master who repays those under his power only with death. Such wages are earned; death is deserved by the servants of sin. It required no inspired apostle to make this statement. It is attested by every human conscience and by the universal experience of men. Sooner or later in the heart of every sinner there reechoes the sad refrain, "The wages of sin is death."

However, "the free gift of God is eternal life in Christ Jesus our Lord." These words which close the chapter come like a revelation from above. "Eternal life" is offered to all. It is not described by the term "wages." It cannot be earned. It can be received only as "the free gift of God." It is for all those who put their trust in

Christ, who are united with him by faith, who in reality are "in Christ Jesus our Lord."

### 3. FREE FROM LAW AND UNITED WITH CHRIST
### Ch. 7:1-6

*1 Or are ye ignorant, brethren (for I speak to men who know the law), that the law hath dominion over a man for so long time as he liveth? 2 For the woman that hath a husband is bound by law to the husband while he liveth; but if the husband die, she is discharged from the law of the husband. 3 So then if, while the husband liveth, she be joined to another man, she shall be called an adulteress: but if the husband die, she is free from the law, so that she is no adulteress, though she be joined to another man. 4 Wherefore, my brethren, ye also were made dead to the law through the body of Christ; that ye should be joined to another, even to him who was raised from the dead, that we might bring forth fruit unto God. 5 For when we were in the flesh, the sinful passions, which were through the law, wrought in our members to bring forth fruit unto death. 6 But now we have been discharged from the law, having died to that wherein we were held; so that we serve in newness of the spirit, and not in oldness of the letter.*

Paul is still defending the doctrine of justification by faith against the supposed objection that it allows sin. The supposition is that if a man be declared just without the works of the law, then he is free to break the law. Paul declares, on the contrary, that justification by faith issues in a life of holiness, and that justification and sanctification are inseparable. He shows that by faith in Christ one is severed from his sin-stained past and is turned with radiant hope toward a new and holy life. He has in the preceding chapter drawn an illustration from the institution of slavery, and has shown that one who is united to Christ has been delivered from the bondage of sin and has been made a servant of righteousness. In this paragraph he is using the illustration of marriage, and is showing that by faith in Christ one is dead to the former influences of the law and is so united with the living Christ as to produce conduct pleasing unto God. Thus he shows that the life of faith is a life of freedom both from sin and the law, yet it is a life of purity and holiness and spiritual power.

In here dealing with the matter of law, Paul addresses particularly the Jewish converts or others who like them were familiar with the revealed law of God. He lays down the familiar principle that "the law hath dominion over a man for so long time as he liveth." Law is limited, however, by life. Its dominion is ended by death. Only while one lives is one bound by the law. Under this general principle Paul gives a specific example. It is that of a woman who is bound by the law during the lifetime of her husband, "but if the husband die, she is discharged from the law of the husband." That is to say, she dies to that law, she is freed from that law, "so that she is no adulteress, though she be joined to another man." In like manner, Paul insists, those who are "made dead to the law through the body of Christ" are free to be united with the risen Christ in a blessed union which will result in "fruit unto God." This death to the law through the body of Christ refers to the experience of those who trust in the work of the crucified Savior as the ground of their acceptance with God and have no confidence in their own righteousness or in the good deeds which they have done. Upon them the law has no claims; even as upon obedience to it they base no hopes. They have been crucified with Christ and so are dead to all the rebukes and the demands of the law. The result is that such believers can be joined in vital union to him who was raised from the grave.

The issue of such a union with Christ is contrasted with the results of the former alliance with law. "For when we were in the flesh," writes Paul, "the sinful passions, which were through the law, wrought in our members to bring forth fruit unto death." That is, before our acceptance of

Christ, while we were in bondage to sin and were under the power of the law, those passions which result in sin and which are aroused and strengthened by the law itself, acted upon the powers of body and of mind to produce results which led only to death.

By way of contrast, Paul declares that "now we have been discharged from the law, having died to that wherein we were held; so that we serve in newness of the spirit, and not in oldness of the letter." That is to say, our release from the law, our death to it as a way of securing acceptance with God, our freedom from its commands and its condemnation, have enabled us to render God a new service which is spiritual in its essence and not mere attempted obedience to an ancient code. It is service through the power of a living Christ and not a mere human and hopeless endeavor to conform to a written statute.

The main message of this paragraph is perfectly clear. It is true, however, that there exist the most widely divergent interpretations of Paul's illustration from marriage. Many writers, in fact, treat the illustration rather as an allegory. They regard the "husband" in the illustration as our corrupt nature and the "wife" as our real and higher self. When, therefore, the old nature, or as Paul uses the phrase, our "old man" dies, the soul is free to marry another, even Christ. Still other interpreters regard the wife as the Christian church. In spite of these divergent views, the essential truth is the same. Paul wishes us to understand that if we are to attain holiness and virtue, it can never be through any attempted obedience to external law, but rather by vital union with the living Christ.

### 4. THE INWARD STRUGGLE   Ch. 7:7-25

*7 What shall we say then? Is the law sin? God forbid. Howbeit, I had not known sin, except through the law: for I had not known coveting, except the law had said, Thou shalt not covet: 8 but sin, finding occasion, wrought in me through the commandment all manner of coveting: for apart from the law sin is dead. 9 And I was alive apart from the law once: but when the commandment came, sin revived, and I died; 10 and the commandment, which was unto life, this I found to be unto death: 11 for sin, finding occasion, through the commandment beguiled me, and through it slew me. 12 So that the law is holy, and the commandment holy, and righteous, and good. 13 Did then that which is good become death unto me? God forbid. But sin, that it might be shown to be sin, by working death to me through that which is good;—that through the commandment sin might become exceeding sinful. 14 For we know that the law is spiritual: but I am carnal, sold under sin. 15 For that which I do I know not: for not what I would, that do I practise; but what I hate, that I do. 16 But if what I would not, that I do, I consent unto the law that it is good. 17 So now it is no more I that do it, but sin which dwelleth in me. 18 For I know that in me, that is, in my flesh, dwelleth no good thing: for to will is present with me, but to do that which is good is not. 19 For the good which I would I do not: but the evil which I would not, that I practise. 20 But if what I would not, that I do, it is no more I that do it, but sin which dwelleth in me. 21 I find then the law, that, to me who would do good, evil is present. 22 For I delight in the law of God after the inward man: 23 but I see a different law in my members, warring against the law of my mind, and bringing me into captivity under the law of sin which is in my members. 24 Wretched man that I am! who shall deliver me out of the body of this death? 25 I thank God through Jesus Christ our Lord. So then I of myself with the mind, indeed, serve the law of God: but with the flesh the law of sin.*

Every man is conscious that conflicting forces of good and evil are contending fiercely for the mastery of his soul. He is ready to confess that in his struggle victory all too seldom rests on the side of the good and that the evil commonly overcomes. Every heart assents to the confession of the ancient poet,

> "Video meliora proboque,
> Deteriora sequor"

("I see the good, and approve it, and yet pursue the wrong"), and also agrees with the verdict of the pagan sage: "He that sins does not do what he would, but what he would not that he does."

This conflict between the lower and the higher self forms the fabric of all drama and all fiction, and of all the tragedy and the misery of human life. No one ever felt this struggle more keenly or painted it so strikingly as the apostle Paul. However, his discussion extends to a realm far higher than that of other writers. He does not depict the struggle merely between the human conscience and the will, in which all men are engaged. He describes, rather, the battle against evil fought by a soul which has been enlightened by the law of God and renewed by the Spirit of God, a battle in which hopeless defeat is turned into victory by the triumphant power of Christ.

The occasion of this matchless passage from the pen of the apostle is his defense of the doctrine of justification by faith. Three possible objections are proposed: First, that it encourages sin (ch. 6:1); second, that it allows sin (ch. 6:15). Paul replies that, on the contrary, true faith in Christ delivers the believer from bondage to both sin and the law. This leads to a third supposed objection: If one declares that in order to lead a holy life it is necessary to be delivered from the law, this is to make the law an evil and an unholy thing. "What shall we say then? Is the law sin?" (Ch. 7:7.) "God forbid," cries the apostle; and then he proceeds to show that the law is good in its own sphere and for its proper purpose. It was designed to reveal sin, not to relieve from sin. It can give relief neither to the soul suffering under the conviction of sin (vs. 7-13), nor to the soul struggling against the power of sin (vs. 14-25).

In each of these two instances Paul phrases his reply in the form of a personal experience. Nothing could be more vivid; yet, while so peculiarly individual, nothing could be more universal in its application. Paul reverts in memory to a time, when, as a proud young Pharisee, he was at ease, confident that he was keeping the law of God because he was so carefully observing its outward forms. However, there came a day when there dawned on his mind the full spiritual meaning of the law, specifically of the commandment, "Thou shalt not covet." The result was twofold. First, it revealed to Paul how much of evil desire really lay lurking in his heart. This he never before had realized. There was, however, an even more terrible result. The very command, "Thou shalt not," made him the more eager to do the thing forbidden. Before the commandment came, sin was "dead"; it was comparatively dormant, inert, and inoperative; but when the commandment came, it gave an impulse to sin. "Sin revived, and I died," that is, I died to my complacent self-satisfaction. I died to true holiness and happiness and hope; I fell deeper and deeper into guilt; I faced only misery and doom and eternal death.

Paul states here a distressing law of human perversity, namely, that a knowledge of right, and a command to obey, instead of producing virtue, are strong incentives to vice. As an old Roman writer declared: "We always endeavor to obtain that which is forbidden, and desire that which is denied," or, as another confessed: "The permitted is unpleasing; the forbidden consumes us fiercely."

Does this prove the moral law to be an evil thing? By no means. The law is "life"; obedience to it would issue in purity and happiness and peace. The law is "holy" and "righteous" and "good." It is no fault or defect of the law that it is the occasion of conviction and of condemnation. The whole fault lies in man, and in the principle of sin, which really works the disaster. So, Paul declares, in his case, sin was allowed to work out its deadly result in order that sin might be made to appear in all its horrid and hideous character. No, the law cannot relieve of sin, but by it sin is revealed (vs. 7-13).

Nor can the law deliver one who is struggling against sin—not even one who has accepted Christ as a Savior,

unless one, looking away from the law and ceasing to
trust in his own ability to keep the law, will cast himself
wholly upon the saving power of Christ.   The trouble
again is not with the law: "For we know that the law is
spiritual," it is pure and holy, the very gift of God.   The
trouble lies with poor, weak human nature.   "But I am
carnal," writes the apostle, under the power of bodily appetites and lusts, "sold under sin," like a captive in war
sold into the service of a cruel tyrant who denies to his vic-
tim all freedom and all power of self-control.   This Paul
makes clear by describing the conflict he has known in
fighting against the evil tendencies and appetites which
continue to strive for mastery over the soul even of a Christian.   This description is measurably true of every human
being who is conscious of the struggle between the higher
and the lower self; but Paul is here describing himself as a
servant of Christ, as one who delights in the law of God,
as one who really wishes to do good.   Even he finds in
himself "a law," a compelling power, bringing him as a
captive under the dominance of sin.   In himself, in his
nature aside from the influence of God, there is "no good
thing"; at least, he is so powerless that, do what he will
and love virtue as he may, still he finds his experience to
be such as he describes in the classic phrase: "The good
which I would I do not: but the evil which I would not,
that I practise."   No amount of knowledge, no effort of
the will, are sufficient to give victory over sin.   "Wretched
man that I am!" cries the apostle; "who shall deliver me
out of the body of this death?"   Who can set him free
from those evil appetites and desires which use as their
instrument this human body with its weaknesses and its
lust, and bring one now and ever under the power of
death? Like a shout of triumph comes the reply: "I thank
God through Jesus Christ our Lord."   The thanksgiving is
offered through Christ, but it is because through him, and
him alone, victory is assured.

Then Paul summarizes the solemn message of this section (vs. 14-25) by declaring that as long as a Christian trusts only in his own unaided powers and seeks thus to keep the law of God, no matter how truly he may love that law, he is certain to be defeated in his struggle for virtue, and to be sold as a captive to sin. "So then I of myself with the mind, indeed, serve the law of God; but with the flesh the law of sin." Victory is possible only through faith in Christ. He alone can make us conquerors; and to him be all the praise.

## 5. LIFE IN THE SPIRIT    Ch. 8:1-17

### a. The Possibility of Holiness    Ch. 8:1-11

*1 There is therefore now no condemnation to them that are in Christ Jesus. 2 For the law of the Spirit of life in Christ Jesus made me free from the law of sin and of death. 3 For what the law could not do, in that it was weak through the flesh, God, sending his own Son in the likeness of sinful flesh and for sin, condemned sin in the flesh: 4 that the ordinance of the law might be fulfilled in us, who walk not after the flesh, but after the Spirit. 5 For they that are after the flesh mind the things of the flesh; but they that are after the Spirit the things of the Spirit. 6 For the mind of the flesh is death; but the mind of the Spirit is life and peace: 7 because the mind of the flesh is enmity against God; for it is not subject to the law of God, neither indeed can it be: 8 and they that are in the flesh cannot please God. 9 But ye are not in the flesh but in the Spirit, if so be that the Spirit of God dwelleth in you. But if any man hath not the Spirit of Christ, he is none of his. 10 And if Christ is in you, the body is dead because of sin; but the spirit is life because of righteousness. 11 But if the Spirit of him that raised up Jesus from the dead dwelleth in you, he that raised up Christ Jesus from the dead shall give life also to your mortal bodies through his Spirit that dwelleth in you.*

If the Epistle of Paul to the Romans rightly has been called "the cathedral of the Christian faith," then surely the eighth chapter may be regarded as its most sacred shrine, or its high altar of worship, of praise, and of prayer. Its splendors are all the more striking because, as readers, we have just emerged from the darkness and the terror of the seventh chapter, with its experiences of moral failure and defeat. However, as we were leaving that dark chamber, there fell on us a dazzling ray of heavenly light promising deliverance through Christ; here, we stand in the full liberty of the children of God, and enjoy a prospect of that glory of God which someday we are to share.

Thus this chapter centers our attention upon two great realities, both secured by the Spirit of God: first, the power for holy living (vs. 1-17), and second, the hope of eternal glory (vs. 18-39); and these two are very closely related, for the power of the Spirit, which enables believers to be holy, is an earnest of their heavenly inheritance.

The presence of this power, therefore, makes holiness possible (vs. 1-11), and for this very reason, makes it more plainly an obligation and a duty (vs. 12-17).

The first sentence of the chapter turns the thought back over the truths already traversed and indicates that here the structure of the epistle is reaching its climax and its crown: "There is therefore now no condemnation to them that are in Christ Jesus." This freedom from "condemnation," this justification, is "by faith," as has been shown by all the chapters which precede; or, to use the expression here employed, it is "to them that are in Christ Jesus." To be "in Christ Jesus" is to enjoy that vital union with him which, on the part of the believer, means trust, obedience, submission, love. The result first mentioned is the "justification" of which Paul has been writing; but other results are to be mentioned, such as the indwelling of the Holy Spirit and all the consequent train of blessings.

This freedom from condemnation refers to: (1) past sins, (2) the possession of a sinful nature, (3) the possibility of overcoming sin.

(1) There is little possibility of holiness until one has

the joyful assurance that his sins have been forgiven and that he has peace with God (ch. 5:1). Pilgrim makes little progress until he reaches the cross and feels the burden of his sins roll away.

(2) Many Christians, however, need to be assured that guilt no longer rests upon them because of the sinful nature of which they are so painfully conscious. Christ Jesus has atoned for our sin as well as for our sins, and if we are in him, then, though we know the evil of our own hearts, we can rejoice in our present acceptance with God.

(3) Nor need the sinful nature of a believer be allowed to express itself in sinful acts, which would bring one under condemnation. Holiness is possible. Each one can truthfully apply to himself the words of Paul: "For the law of the Spirit of life in Christ Jesus made me free from the law of sin and of death."

By the word "law," Paul here means not the law of Moses but the power, the operation, the influence of the Holy Spirit, who delivers the believer from the power or dominion of the tyrant, "Sin," and from his dread awards, or "wages," namely, "death." By way of contrast, the Spirit here is called "the Spirit of life," for he is the Author of love and joy and peace and holiness and eternal life. Not by struggling in our own strength can we live holy lives, but by the power of the Spirit, as we appropriate to ourselves all that has been secured for us by Christ. He has made provision whereby we are enabled to keep the law of God, and in him holiness is possible: "For what the law could not do, in that it was weak through the flesh, God, sending his own Son in the likeness of sinful flesh and for sin, condemned sin in the flesh: that the ordinance of the law might be fulfilled in us, who walk not after the flesh, but after the Spirit."

The reason why the law could not condemn sin and make it powerless, was because poor human nature was powerless to resist temptation and was ever inclined to evil. The law could reveal sin and condemn sin, but it was unable to solve the problem of sin. It was "weak" because it was dealing with frail and sinful men. "It was weak through the flesh."

God, however, brought deliverance, by "sending his own Son," who assumed human nature with all its characteristics, excepting its sinfulness. Thus he came "in the likeness of sinful flesh." He came "for sin," that is, to expiate sin, and quite as truly to expel sin. "In the flesh," that is, by taking upon himself human nature, yet denying to sin any power over him, and finally, by his death, he "condemned sin," revealed its true nature, deposed it from its dominion, and delivered from its thralldom all who put their trust in him, so that, in his death, believers have at once the ground of pardon and the pledge of purity. The great purpose of his mission, therefore, was that "the ordinance of the law," the just requirement of the Mosaic moral code, "might be fulfilled in us."

This is possibly the strongest, fullest, clearest statement in reference to the doctrine of justification by faith that the apostle has made. Contrary to all the supposed objections, this method of justification, neither encouraging sin nor allowing sin, nor making the law a sinful thing, was the only possible method by which sinful men could overcome sin and obey the law. The very purpose of justification is sanctification. The very end in view, according to God's way of saving men, is the complete fulfillment of all that the law of God demands. This fulfillment of the law can be made, however, only by those "who walk not after the flesh, but after the Spirit," that is, who live not according to the corrupt passions and evil inclinations of human nature but according to the guidance and the regulating power of the Holy Spirit.

The necessity for walking according to the Spirit is evident from the contrast between these two modes of life. Persons who yield to the appeal and are under the influence of sinful desires, think of, and care for, and seek to obtain only those things which belong to the flesh; while

those who "walk after the Spirit" have their practical interests in the sphere of the things that are spiritual.

The results are quite as different. Of the one it is
"death," both of the soul and the body; of the other, it is
"life," and a sense of harmony and peace with God. In
fact, it is particularly in their relation to God that these
two modes of life are most contrasted. Those that are "in
the flesh" are hostile to God, disobedient to God, and incapable of obeying God.

On the contrary, Christians are under the influence not
of the "flesh" but of the Spirit, because the Spirit of God
dwells in them. This is true of every Christian. All may
not yield themselves in equal measure to the influence of
the Spirit; some may more frequently grieve him and disobey him; but he never leaves the Christian. To speak of
a Christian who has not the abiding presence of the Holy
Spirit is a contradiction in terms: "But if any man hath
not the Spirit of Christ, he is none of his" (v. 9).

Therefore the presence of the Holy Spirit is attended
with blessed results, for while the body of a believer is still
subject to the law of death and certain in time to die, yet
his spirit is instinct with a new and heavenly life because
of the very fact of the righteousness which has been received by faith. Not only so, but the presence of the Holy
Spirit is an earnest and pledge of the resurrection of the
body; for if the Spirit of God "that raised up Christ Jesus
from the dead" dwells in the believer, then surely God
will raise from the dead the body of the believer. Of this
certain resurrection the Spirit may be regarded as the
Agent ("through his Spirit"), or more probably the Pledge
("because of his Spirit," v. 11, margin); for a body which
has been sanctified as a temple of the Holy Spirit will not
be left permanently under the power of death, but will be
raised in immortal glory. Such a glorious destiny of spirit
and of body awaits all those who are "in Christ Jesus."

### b. The Duty of Holiness   Ch. 8:12-17

12 So then, brethren, we are debtors, not to the flesh, to
live after the flesh: 13 for if ye live after the flesh, ye must
die; but if by the Spirit ye put to death the deeds of the
body, ye shall live.  14 For as many as are led by the Spirit
of God, these are sons of God.  15 For ye received not the
spirit of bondage again unto fear; but ye received the spirit
of adoption, whereby we cry, Abba, Father.  16 The Spirit
himself beareth witness with our spirit, that we are children
of God: 17 and if children, then heirs; heirs of God, and
joint-heirs with Christ; if so be that we suffer with him,
that we may be also glorified with him.

Two opposite tendencies are manifested by Christians
in the matter of holy living.  Some grow indifferent and
fall back under the slavery of sin; others strive to do right
only because they are afraid to do wrong, and they stand
in constant dread of God whom they serve in the attitude
of slaves.  Against both of these tendencies Paul warns
his readers, as he reminds them that holiness is a duty, and
that it can be attained only by allowing the Holy Spirit
to rule the life, as one lives in trustful fellowship with God
as his loving Father and looks forward to a heavenly inheritance in glory.

Paul has been setting forth the high privilege of Christians for whom holiness has been made possible by the
incarnation and the saving work of the Son of God, and
by the indwelling power of the Spirit of God.

However, high privilege always involves grave responsibility.  If holiness has been made possible for Christians
at so great cost, and if they have been called also to a
heavenly destiny, then surely, for every Christian, holiness
is a duty, an obligation, a debt.

"So then, brethren, we are debtors, not to the flesh, to
live after the flesh."  To the old life of sin, to its evil passions and appetites and indulgences, we owe no debt of
obedience.  Our real debt is to the Spirit who empowers

us for holy living, to whom therefore we owe submission and service. If we live according to the "flesh," we shall not fulfill the glorious destiny Paul described when assuring believers of that future glory in which even their bodies are to share. "For if ye live after the flesh, ye must die; but if by the Spirit ye put to death the deeds of the body, ye shall live." These "deeds of the body," these sins to which we are tempted by our bodily appetites, must be done to death by the power of the Holy Spirit. Every day has its battles for a follower of Christ, every hour its struggle; but by trustful surrender to the Holy Spirit, constant victory can be enjoyed. Then in the truest sense we "shall live."

This is so because all who "are led by the Spirit of God, these are sons of God"; they enjoy life in its fullness, they are objects of his special favor. This relation to God as his "sons" implies a trustful intimacy. As Christians, we have "received not the spirit of bondage again unto fear," not such a spirit as might rule a slave, a spirit of dread and terror, such a spirit as possibly we felt before when we were living under law or possibly under the mastery of sin. On the contrary, we have "received the spirit of adoption," a spirit which inspires and befits those who have been adopted as sons. In such a spirit of filial trust and confidence and love, we draw near to God in prayer, and cry, "Abba, Father." The Aramaic word for father, "Abba," was on the lips of our Lord in the hour of his agony, and became familiar to all believers, so that the added word, "Father," is here less like a translation or an explanation than a repetition, the repetition of a child crying, "Father, father, O father!"

To such a consciousness of nearness, of acceptance, and of affection, the Spirit himself adds his own witness, assuring us, even as our own spirit assures us, that we, who are all that is implied by the word "sons" are also "children of God." "Sons" is the term more commonly employed by Paul. It denotes a legal relationship, one of privilege and of right.   "Children" is the term more usual in the writings of John, and denotes kinship, nature, birth, origin.   Strictly speaking, one becomes a "son" by adoption, a "child" by a "new birth."   We have received a spirit of trust and fellowship, befitting those who have been brought into the family of God by his gracious adoption; yet it is also the spirit of those who realize their vital relation to God as his own children, born of his Spirit.

Here, however, the relations of law and of kinship are closely united; for Paul at once argues that "if children, then heirs; heirs of God, and joint-heirs with Christ." According to Roman law, though not Jewish, all children, including adopted children, received equal shares of an inheritance.   Thus, as his "sons," we are to share the heavenly glory of God; as his "children," we are to partake more and more fully of his divine nature.

To such an inheritance, however, a condition is here attached: "If so be that we suffer with him, that we may be also glorified with him" (v. 17).   These sufferings are probably not merely the trials and distresses incident to all human life, but rather, the hardships and sacrifices and persecutions we suffer for the sake of Christ, and specifically in his service.   Those who thus suffer, or who endure all distresses patiently as his servants, will surely share his heavenly glory, a glory he had with the Father "before the world was."

Holiness, then, is a duty.   It is not merely a privilege of the few, but because the privilege of all, it is an obligation for all; and this obligation is emphasized by the facts here set forth, namely, that as the sons of God, believers are guided by his Spirit, they enjoy fellowship with him as their Father, they are joint heirs with his Son.   Surely such considerations as these cannot fail to make them eager to fulfill more perfectly their obligation to lead holy lives.

### 6. PATIENCE IN SUFFERING     Ch. 8:18-30

*a. The Hope of Glory     Ch. 8:18-25*

*18 For I reckon that the sufferings of this present time are not worthy to be compared with the glory which shall be revealed to us-ward. 19 For the earnest expectation of the creation waiteth for the revealing of the sons of God. 20 For the creation was subjected to vanity, not of its own will, but by reason of him who subjected it, in hope 21 that the creation itself also shall be delivered from the bondage of corruption into the liberty of the glory of the children of God. 22 For we know that the whole creation groaneth and travaileth in pain together until now. 23 And not only so, but ourselves also, who have the first-fruits of the Spirit, even we ourselves groan within ourselves, waiting for* our *adoption,* to wit, *the redemption of our body. 24 For in hope were we saved: but hope that is seen is not hope: for who hopeth for that which he seeth? 25 But if we hope for that which we see not,* then *do we with patience wait for it.*

Paul is always a prophet, in the sense that he speaks for God to men; occasionally, however, he prophesies in the more popular sense of predicting future events. This he does with no such mention of details as to cast doubt upon the fulfillment, but rather, with such dignity and reserve as to argue divine guidance and authority. Evidently his purpose never is to gratify idle curiosity or to indulge in fruitless dreams. His intention is always practical. He seeks either to inspire purity of life or patience in suffering, or to justify the dealings of God with men.

Twice in this chapter he has mentioned the future glory of believers, but only in references which were logically related to his argument. First, in speaking of the sanctifying power of the indwelling Spirit, he concludes that his presence in believers is a pledge of the resurrection of their bodies (v. 11); and second, in describing the sonship of believers, he argues that this assures their share in the heavenly glory of Christ (v. 17).

In this second instance, however, he adds a condition: those who are to share the glory of Christ must first share his sufferings; and all that Paul adds as to future glory is designed to make Christians patient in present sufferings.

The first reason he assigned for such patience is the surpassing greatness of the glory: "For I reckon that the sufferings of this present time are not worthy to be compared with the glory which shall be revealed to us-ward" (v. 18). Paul has just stated that the path to glory lies through pain. But what of that, he is now saying, "For the pain is not worth a thought in view of the radiant splendor which some day will break through the dark clouds to surround and transfigure us." "I reckon" denotes not doubt but a confident assurance. "The sufferings of this present time" include all the persecutions and trials and distresses and afflictions which are endured for the sake of Christ. "The glory" is that which is to transform the bodies and the souls of believers at the coming, the future appearing, of Christ.

That glory is certain to appear. "The revealing of the sons of God," their future manifestation in heavenly splendor, is absolutely assured. One proof is seen in the expectant attitude of all nature, turned eagerly toward that predicted event in the glory of which nature itself is to have a share. "For the earnest expectation of the creation waiteth for the revealing of the sons of God." (V. 19.)

With arresting boldness of poetic imagery, Paul personifies all animate and inanimate creation. Centuries ago all nature was condemned to disappointment, to a sense of futility and emptiness, was made a slave to decay and corruption, "was subjected to vanity." This was contrary to "its own will"; it was due to no fault of its own; God fixed this doom upon it. But at the same time he inspired the hope, that, as nature had been made to share in the bondage of corruption because of the fall and sin of man, so, too, it yet would partake of the freedom from evil and decay which constitute the future "glory of the children of God." (Vs. 20-21.) The very groans and travail pains of universal nature are prophetic not of death but of new life: they are the birth throes of a better order of things. (V. 22.) Paul thus teaches not the destruction but the renewal of nature. He indicates that its present is neither its original nor its final state, but the present contains the prophecy of a more glorious future.

The experience of Christians points in the same direction. These sighs of irrational creation are shared by the sons of God, whose very groans are prophetic of the glory which yet is to be theirs. For we are sighing for that full harvest of blessedness of which the Spirit is the first fruit and earnest. Just because we have this pledge, we yearn only more intensely for the complete realization of our "adoption, which will consist in the redemption of our body." For when our bodies are delivered from death by resurrection, or by instant transformation at the appearing of Christ, then our glory will be complete (v. 23).

Such an expectation of completed "adoption" on the part of Christians is in perfect keeping with the conditions under which they accepted salvation. They accepted it not in complete possession but also in prospect; not as a fully accomplished reality, but, so far as the body and external conditions were concerned, as a hope: "For in hope were we saved." Our salvation, thus, from the first, was qualified with a hope of blessings yet to be ours. Had the object we longed for already been realized, hope would have ceased to exist. "Hope that is seen is not hope." As our perfect blessedness is future, we cannot expect to enjoy it now. However, in view of this future "revealing of the sons of God," we wait in earnest expectation, and learn what it is to be patient in suffering.

### b. The Divine Help and Purpose    Ch. 8:26-30

26 And in like manner the Spirit also helpeth our infirmity: for we know not how to pray as we ought; but the Spirit himself maketh intercession for us with groanings

*which cannot be uttered; 27 and he that searcheth the*
*hearts knoweth what is the mind of the Spirit, because he*
*maketh intercession for the saints according to the will of*
*God.   28 And we know that to them that love God all*
*things work together for good, even to them that are called*
*according to his purpose.   29 For whom he foreknew, he*
*also foreordained to be conformed to the image of his Son,*
*that he might be the firstborn among many brethren: 30*
*and whom he foreordained, them he also called: and whom*
*he called, them he also justified: and whom he justified,*
*them he also glorified.*

Against a dark background of present suffering, Paul
has been depicting the future glory of believers; he has
been encouraging them to be patient in their suffering because of the surpassing greatness of the coming glory.
Here he adds two further reasons for patience, namely, the
help being given by the Spirit of God and the knowledge
of the loving purpose of God.

"And in like manner," that we, in spite of our sighs and
sufferings, may "with patience wait" for the promised
glory, "the Spirit also helpeth our infirmity"—our natural
weakness which might make us faint and despair under the
trial and delay.   There is one particular form of help which
Christians all need, and which Paul proceeds to specify,
namely, help in prayer: "For we know not how to pray
as we ought"—we are ignorant of the right content and
form of prayer.   This is one of the most common and
conscious of our limitations; "but the Spirit himself maketh
intercession for us with groanings which cannot be uttered."   This intercession of the Spirit is not apart from,
but in and through, our consciousness.   As Augustine said,
"Not in himself, and with himself, but in us he groans, for
he makes us groan."   He inspires in our hearts yearnings
and aspirations and desires which are too deep for words.
(V. 26.)

However, these prayers, so imperfectly expressed, are
certain to be heard and answered, for "he that searcheth

the hearts knoweth what is the mind of the Spirit, because he maketh intercession for the saints according to the will of God." "He that searcheth the hearts" is a phrase that well might fill us with fear, but here it is designed to give comfort and hope. In spite of all our failure and weakness and discouragement, God looks down deep into our hearts and he sees there the secret and unexpressed desires for holiness and happiness and glory which his own Spirit has inspired, and he interprets these sighs, breathed into our hearts by his Spirit, as prayers offered for his own people, and in accordance with his own will. Surely in no experience of life can we rely upon divine aid more confidently than when in the exercise of prayer; and when we feel even too weak to pray, we can rest confident that a divine Intercessor, a Helper, a Comforter, is voicing the longings we lack strength to express.

A third reason (vs. 18, 26) for patiently enduring suffering with Christ, for his sake, and in his cause, is found in the conviction, held in common by all Christians, "that to them that love God all things work together for good" (v. 28). Few statements of Scripture are more familiar than this, or more full of comfort. Some ancient manuscripts introduce the word "God" a second time in this brief phrase: "And we know that God cooperates for good in all things with those that love him." In both cases the meaning is the same. All things work together for good not by inherent force, not by fate or chance, but by divine control. Thus not only does the divine Spirit help us in our weakness, but divine Providence works with us "for good in all things." This comforting conviction is strengthened by experience and observation, but it is founded upon faith in the constant care of a loving Father. The "all things" refers first to sufferings, and the "good" to future "glory"; but we need not restrict the meaning. No experience incident to human life should be regarded as beyond the permission and power of God, or incapable of being used by him to promote our truest "good."

There is one restriction, however. This "good" is "to them," or this cooperation for good is with them only "that love God." All things worth mentioning are against those who do not love him, all his holiness and his justice and his power and his changeless law and his eternal judgment; but those who seek to do his will, those who accept his salvation, those who rest in his grace, can be sure of his loving care in the darkness as well as in the light, and can know that through all the mysteries of life he is perfecting a plan of eternal glory.

To strengthen our faith further, Paul describes those who, from the human point of view, "love God," as those who, from the divine side, "are called according to his purpose"; and then he states five successive steps by which this divine "purpose" is being carried into effect. (1) It includes an act of divine intelligence reaching back into eternity; even then God "foreknew" us and regarded us with favor. (2) It is expressed also as an act of the divine will: "Whom he foreknew, he also foreordained to be conformed to the image of his Son"; so that believers are destined ultimately to bear the moral and spiritual likeness of their Master and Lord. The final purpose of this foreordaining, or predestinating act, is the glory of the Lord, "that he might be the firstborn among many brethren"; for the supreme glory of Christ consists in the salvation of that brotherhood of the redeemed among whom he stands forth as the supreme and the unique "Son of the Father." (3) This gracious purpose, formed in eternity, is carried out in time by a divine call given by his Spirit to those for whom God has such a destiny in store. (4) "And whom he called, them he also justified"—he freely forgave their sins and declared them to be righteous. (5) "And whom he justified, them he also glorified." That past tense, "glorified," in reference to an experience which at least in its fullness is still future, has been termed "amazing," "the most daring anticipation of faith that even the New Testament contains"; but the future glory of believers is a present reality in the mind and purpose of God. Some foregleams of that glory they already enjoy, and its hope is so assured that through all this chapter it is being emphasized, to encourage patience in suffering on the part of those who are "heirs of God, and joint-heirs with Christ."

In all this majestic movement whereby these successive stages of the divine purpose are carried into effect, nothing is stated as to the agency or activity or responsibility of believers. Here the thought is of God. That Paul also believed and taught the freedom of the human will, the responsibility of man, and the need of repentance and faith and love, must not be forgotten. Nor does he ever seek to reconcile these two spheres of truth. However, in seeking to encourage us to patience in suffering and to confident expectation of future glory, he wisely fixes the attention wholly upon that which must be ultimate in all our thinking and our thanksgiving, namely, upon the mysterious, loving, eternal purpose of God.

### 7. THE ASSURANCE OF SALVATION    Ch. 8:31-39

31 What then shall we say to these things? If God is for us, who is against us? 32 He that spared not his own Son, but delivered him up for us all, how shall he not also with him freely give us all things? 33 Who shall lay anything to the charge of God's elect? It is God that justifieth; 34 who is he that condemneth? It is Christ Jesus that died, yea rather, that was raised from the dead, who is at the right hand of God, who also maketh intercession for us. 35 Who shall separate us from the love of Christ? shall tribulation, or anguish, or persecution, or famine, or nakedness, or peril, or sword? 36 Even as it is written,

For thy sake we are killed all the day long;
We were accounted as sheep for the slaughter.
37 Nay, in all these things we are more than conquerors through him that loved us. 38 For I am persuaded, that neither death, nor life, nor angels, nor principalities, nor things present, nor things to come, nor powers, 39 nor

*height, nor depth, nor any other creature, shall be able to*
*separate us from the love of God, which is in Christ Jesus*
*our Lord.*

This is probably the most majestic passage which has
come to us from the apostle Paul.  It is the climax of his
argument.  He has shown that believers in Christ are justified by faith, that their justification results in holy living
and finally issues in eternal glory.  Now follow this triumphant hymn which voices for believers their confident
assurance of salvation.  For them there can be no loss
(vs. 31-32); upon them can rest no condemnation (vs.
33-34); to them can come no separation from the love of
God in Christ Jesus (vs. 35-39).

There is, however, an immediate connection between
this "paean of exultant praise" and the verses which immediately precede.  Paul has been tracing the successive
steps by which God carries out his eternal purpose toward
them that love him.  "What then," asks the apostle, "shall
we say to these things?"  In view of this divine plan of
mercy, what conclusion can we draw other than that of
comfort and of confidence?  There can be no doubt of the
power of God; no enemy can withstand his purpose: "If
God is for us, who is against us?"  Nor can there be any
doubt of God's love.  As Abraham spared not Isaac, so
he "spared not his own Son," his only Son, the One who
alone shared his divine being.  Is this not absolute proof
that he is ready to "freely give us all things" needed for
our salvation?  As he is able, so he surely is willing
to save.  There then can be no loss for the believer.
(Vs. 31-32.)

Nor can there be any condemnation.  Even of believers
it is true that "conscience does make cowards of us all,"
in the sense that we are made fearful and despondent and
ashamed as we remember our failures and faults and sins;
but if God has declared that we belong to him, and if he
has pronounced us just, what accusation need be feared:

"Who shall lay anything to the charge of God's elect? It is God that justifieth."

Likewise, as no one can reopen the case against us, so, too, no contrary verdict need be feared. Christ is our Defender, our Advocate, our Savior, our Hope, "who is he that condemneth?" If we have sinned, Christ died for our sins, and his resurrection is a pledge and proof of our acquittal; if we feel our weakness before temptations, we remember that he is in the place of supreme power "at the right hand of God"; and, also, in virtue of his atoning work he ever "maketh intercession for us." As our trust is in him, we allow our souls to be distressed by no terrors from the past. (Vs. 33-34.)

Nor does the prospect of the future fill us with fear. Nothing it may bring can separate us from the love of Christ. "Shall tribulation, or anguish, or persecution, or famine, or nakedness, or peril, or sword?" Surely, for Paul and his friends in Rome, these were no empty words. They knew so well, and were yet to know, what it means to suffer for the sake of their Lord that they could well apply to themselves the description, given by the inspired psalmist, of innocent sufferers in his day:

"For thy sake we are killed all the day long;
    We were accounted as sheep for the slaughter."

With all these things in view, so certain was Paul of the unfailing love of Christ, that he could exclaim, "Nay, in all these things we are more than conquerors through him that loved us." In just what particular we can be "more than conquerors" Paul leaves us to conjecture; whether in "the overwhelming defeat of our enemies," or in our "surpassing" or "triumphant victory," or in our "unconquerable strength," he does not say; possibly he means that all these trials only give us more thrilling experiences of the love of Christ which was manifested in his death for us, and is revealed toward those who live for him.

In any case, Paul confirms this sense of "jubilant triumph" by a statement of his own unalterable conviction that in the whole universe there is nothing which Christian faith need fear. No form or phase of being can break the golden chain that binds the heart of God to his loved ones. Not "death" with its terrors or "life" with its changes; not any condition of existence; not "angels," nor any hierarchy of invisible beings, whether good or evil; nothing within the sweep of time either "present" or "to come," however powerful; nothing in the illimitable spaces above or beneath; nothing in all the vast creation shall be able to sunder us from that divine love which is in Christ Jesus our Lord. Our comfort, our consolation, our blessed assurance of salvation rest, in the last analysis, not upon anything in us, but rather upon the power and steadfastness of almighty love.

## C. THE PROBLEM OF ISRAEL'S REJECTION
### Chs. 9 to 11

The ninth, tenth, and eleventh chapters of the epistle form what is termed a "theodicy," a vindication of God, a justification of his dealings with men.

The particular problem which confronted Paul was the fate of Israel. This was God's chosen people, his elect nation; how, then, could the people of Israel be under the wrath of God, as the epistle has declared them to be? How can this choice of God be reconciled with his condemnation of Israel?

Then, too, through his inspired prophets, God had promised that Israel should be a blessing to all the nations of the earth; this blessing was to consist not merely in giving to the world a Savior, a Messiah, but in accepting this Savior and in fellowship with this Messiah. In fact, however, Israel had rejected Christ, the Savior; and while Israel was being set aside, Gentiles were receiving all the blessings of justification and new life and eternal glory, through faith in Christ. How, then, can the promises of

God be reconciled with the unbelief and consequent rejection of Israel?

In these three chapters Paul makes his reply. First, the promises of God were never intended for all who were Israelites by birth, but for such as were true children of God by faith, and at the present time those who were truly God's chosen people from among both Jews and Gentiles were receiving the greatest of all blessings, the righteousness provided by God. (Ch. 9.)

Secondly, the rejection of Israel as a nation was due entirely to the fault of Israel. The way of salvation appointed by God, even through faith in Christ, was offered to all, and had been made perfectly plain to Israel. Their rejection, therefore, was not arbitrary on the part of God, but was due to their stubborn and willful unbelief. (Ch. 10.)

Thirdly, the rejection of Israel, while only partial, was likewise only temporary. A time would come when Israel as a nation would repent and accept Christ as their Messiah and become a blessing to all the nations of the world. (Ch. 11.)

The nature of this reply, therefore, shows the place which these chapters occupy in the epistle. They are not a digression, not a parenthesis, not an appendix, but a necessary part, indeed the very climax of the argument, the completion of the doctrinal teaching which the epistle sets forth. From the first, Paul had been writing with his Jewish kindred in mind. He had declared his gospel to be "the power of God unto salvation . . . to the Jew first, and also to the Greek." He had demonstrated how much the Jew needed the righteousness which the gospel revealed. He had shown, from the Jewish Scriptures, the way of righteousness by faith. He had answered the various objections which a Jew might make to a righteousness which was "apart from the law." It was absolutely necessary, then, that Paul should deal with the historic and pathetic situation in which the Jews, as a nation, were rejecting the righteousness which God had provided; and further that Paul should show how this present unbelief on the part of Israel was related to the salvation of Gentiles, and how this salvation of Gentiles was destined to stir up Israel to jealousy and to the acceptance of the Messiah. These three chapters, therefore, contain Paul's philosophy of history, and show that the "justification by faith" of which he has been writing is absolutely universal in its application, and that his gospel is yet to bring salvation to all the nations of the world.

These chapters are difficult, possibly the most difficult to interpret of any which Paul ever penned. Their chief obscurities are in connection with his statements of divine sovereignty and "election." It should be noted, however, that he is discussing national conversion and not individual salvation. If the latter were in view, he probably would have been more explicit and comprehensive in his statements.

Then, again, care should be taken to note all that he says even here. It is possible to form quite wrong opinions by reading detached and isolated statements; the three chapters must be read as a unit. Paul does state the sovereignty of God, but also, quite as clearly, the free agency and moral responsibility of man. The three chapters form a trilogy: The first deals with divine sovereignty, the second with human responsibility, the third with universal blessing; the first with "election," the second with "rejection," the third with "restoration"; the first with the past, the second with the present, the third with the future. They open with a cry of anguish as Paul looks upon the unbelief and loss of the kinsmen he so truly loves; they close with a doxology of praise in view of the mercy which overarches all the mysterious providences of God, whose "judgments" are "unsearchable," whose "ways past tracing."

The discussion is intensely practical. Paul makes no endeavor to reconcile the facts of divine predestination and human freedom, nor to explain the relation of the will of God to the will of man. While stating, in startling terms, the sovereignty of God, he nonetheless holds Israel responsible for its impenitent unbelief, and warns the Gentiles against pride, self-confidence, and loss of faith.

In fact, the practical aspect of the discussion is its main feature. Israel is regarded not merely as Israel but as representing all that vast mass of men who in all time are seeking salvation by works of law, by human effort, by a righteousness of their own. The presentation of the doctrine of justification by faith here reaches its climax. The peril and plight of Israel is that of every man who refuses the salvation freely offered through faith in Christ.

God does promise blessings to those who do right and keep his law, but this is divinely conditioned upon faith in him, and upon a heart full of submission and trust, not upon any mere outward conformity to law. (Ch. 9.)

Again, no matter how moral one is trying to be, he is really guilty of fatal fault, if he is willfully refusing the way of goodness and life, of pardon and purity, provided in Jesus Christ. (Ch. 10.)

Then, too, all men will come ultimately to see that God's way of salvation is the only way. Jew and Gentile at last will turn in faith to Christ, and will praise the goodness and grace of God. (Ch. 11.)

It may be added that there is practical help in reading any true theodicy. At times, we all need to have the dealings of God explained. His providences are full of mystery; the fulfillments of his promises are long delayed. We must be encouraged to trust in his sovereign grace, to be faithful and submissive to Christ, and to look forward to a glorious future when at last we shall understand "the riches both of the wisdom and the knowledge of God! . . . To him be the glory for ever. Amen."

## 1. THE REJECTION OF ISRAEL IS NOT COMPLETE
### Ch. 9:1-29

### a. Paul's Sorrow for Israel    Ch. 9:1-5

*1 I say the truth in Christ, I lie not, my conscience bearing witness with me in the Holy Spirit, 2 that I have great sorrow and unceasing pain in my heart. 3 For I could wish that I myself were anathema from Christ for my brethren's sake, my kinsmen according to the flesh: 4 who are Israelites; whose is the adoption, and the glory, and the covenants, and the giving of the law, and the service of God, and the promises; 5 whose are the fathers, and of whom is Christ as concerning the flesh, who is over all, God blessed for ever. Amen.*

The Christian church would never lack converts if all its members or even its ministers felt for their friends and fellow countrymen the deep concern expressed by the apostle Paul for his kinsmen the Jews.

He has been gazing with rapture upon the present blessedness and future glory of Christian believers; and as he now turns to consider the unbelief of his own people, Israel, the contrast causes him to cry out with anguish of heart. He attests the truth of his statement by affirming that he speaks as one whose life is centered "in Christ" and whose "conscience" is under the direct influence of "the Holy Spirit."

The intensity of his feeling is emphasized by describing it as "great sorrow," and as "unceasing pain" of heart. He does not specify the cause of his grief, but leaves it to be implied; and he solemnly attests his sincerity by stating that, if thus he might secure the salvation of his people, he could wish himself "anathema," "accursed," and so separated "from Christ." He does not assert that such a wish is actual or that such an end could be accomplished by such means. Here we must avoid "the error of explaining the language of feeling as though it were that of reasoning and reflection." Paul thus expresses his unmeasured devotion. He was like Moses, who prayed for his guilty people, "Yet now, if thou wilt forgive their sin—; and if not, blot me, I pray thee, out of thy book which thou hast written." So the apostle is expressing his willingness to make any sacrifice to accomplish the salvation of Israel.

He states two grounds for his intense passion. The first is that the Jews are his "brethren," his "kinsmen according to the flesh." They are not members of that even dearer Christian brotherhood which is "according to" the Spirit. Nevertheless, Paul here recognizes and glorifies those human ties of blood and kinship which are ever to be held sacred, which Paul refuses to renounce in spite of the Jewish hatred which has caused him constant pain and peril. He never forgot the claims of nature. He loved his people just because they were his people.

However, there is a second cause for his passionate concern; it consists in the special privileges which have been given to the Jews as the chosen people of God. He cannot endure the thought that those so highly favored are perishing for lack of faith. They are "Israelites," and as bearers of that sacred name, they are partakers of the promises made to Jacob, to whom the name "Israel" was first given. They are the descendants and heirs of Israel: can it be that they are shut off from the blessings God assured to his seed? They are a people in covenant relation with God: has God cast them off?

Theirs is "the adoption," the status of an adopted son, for from among all the nations of the world God chose Israel to be his peculiar people, his "son," his "firstborn" (Ex. 4:22; Hos. 11:1).

Theirs is "the glory," the Shekinah, the visible presence of God in the Tabernacle and in the Temple of old: had this presence been permanently withdrawn?

Theirs are "the covenants," repeatedly renewed, binding them as a people to God. To them had been given "the law," by direct revelation and amid circumstances of peculiar awe and splendor.

Theirs is the Temple "service," a ritual of divine appointment and of unparalleled significance and solemnity.

Theirs are "the promises," pointing forward to a coming Messiah in whom they, and through them all the nations, are to be blest.

Theirs are "the fathers," the ancient Patriarchs, who as saintly ancestors cast a glory over all the generations of Jews.

Last of all, their supreme privilege and distinction is this, that from them has come Christ, of their own blood so far as his assumed humanity is concerned, but in his eternal "being" over all, God blessed for ever."

It is true that many devout scholars prefer to read the last clause as a doxology: He "who is over all, God be blessed forever." If that reading is accepted, still it can be remembered that there are many other New Testament passages which assert the deity of our Lord; but it is probably safe to follow the Authorized and the Revised Versions and to regard this as the most positive statement of the divine nature of Christ found in all the writings of Paul.

Such peculiar privileges, culminating in their gift to the world, even Christ, their promised Messiah, are enough to explain Paul's love for his Jewish kinsmen, and his anguish of heart at their unbelief.

The paragraph, however, serves as an admirable introduction to the three chapters which it opens, for while Paul is to set forth the responsibility and the guilt of Israel, such an opening expression of passionate love disarms any suspicion of prejudice or of hostility on his part; and at the same time, this recital of the high privileges of Israel only emphasizes the problem of Israel's rejection. Each item of the long list indicates that the nation has been chosen of God and is peculiarly precious to him. How can such a people fail to enjoy the salvation which has been provided by God? This is the problem Paul is now to discuss.

However, on turning from this inspired catalog of Jewish privileges, it may be well for Christians to consider how the larger privileges which they enjoy may be associated with these same terms.

The Jews bore the name of "Israelites." What is the fuller and more glorious significance of the name "Christians"? Theirs, as a nation, was "the adoption," but all who accept the gospel message are "heirs of God, and joint-heirs with Christ," and theirs is the spirit of sonship whereby they cry to God, "Abba, Father." Theirs is "the glory" which shines from the face of Jesus Christ, the supreme revelation of God to men. Theirs is a "new covenant" in the blood of Christ, "poured out for many unto remission of sins." Theirs is the gift of the Spirit of God by whose power can be fulfilled "the law" of God. Theirs, too, are "precious and exceeding great promises," by which they "become partakers of the divine nature." Theirs, too, are the "fathers," and they are ever inspired by the consciousness that they belong to the great company of saints, apostles, prophets, martyrs, whose lives have hallowed the earth, with whom they shall be united in heaven. "Christ" is theirs and they are his, and having him they have all things.

Such exalted privileges imply sacred obligations. Should not all Christians feel "great sorrow and unceasing pain" for those whose hearts are hardened, who in blind unbelief are rejecting the salvation of God?

### b. Israel's Rejection and God's Promise   Ch. 9:6-13

6 But it is *not as though the word of God hath come to nought. For they are not all Israel, that are of Israel: 7 neither, because they are Abraham's seed, are they all children: but, In Isaac shall thy seed be called. 8 That is, it is not the children of the flesh that are children of God; but the children of the promise are reckoned for a seed.*

*9 For this is a word of promise, according to this season
will I come, and Sarah shall have a son.   10 And not only
so; but Rebecca also having conceived by one, even by our
Father Isaac—11 for* the children *being not yet born,
neither having done anything good or bad, that the purpose
of God according to election might stand, not of works,
but of him that calleth, 12 it was said unto her, The elder
shall serve the younger.   13 Even as it is written, Jacob I
loved, but Esau I hated.*

Paul has been voicing his sorrow for the people of
Israel, a sorrow deepened by the fact that they are his own
kindred, and further, that they have been the recipients of
divine promises and have enjoyed unparalleled privileges
as the chosen people of God.   He has not stated, however,
the cause of his sorrow.   This has been implied.   His pain
of heart is due to the rejection of Israel; they have been
cast off; they are not receiving the blessings which Gentiles
are enjoying through faith in Christ.   It would seem, then,
that God had broken his promise, that God was unfaithful
to his word.

Paul at once replies that the case is not such, "as though
the word of God hath come to nought," for the promises
made to Israel were never intended for all who were descended from Jacob, any more than the promise made to
Abraham was intended for all his sons.   Among the latter,
Ishmael was older than Isaac, yet when Abraham had
cast forth Hagar and her son, there came to him the divine word, "In Isaac shall thy seed be called."   This shows
that the right to be the children of God and heirs of his
promises does not depend upon the mere accident of birth
but upon the action of the divine will in accordance with
the divine word.   The promise is the important matter,
not mere physical birth.   Thus before Isaac was born,
the promise was made, "According to this season will I
come, and Sarah shall have a son."   Thus Isaac was a
child of promise, born not only in accord with the promise
but because of the will of God which the promise ex-

pressed, and because of Abraham's faith in God which rested on the promise of God.

Therefore, the promises of God to the nation of Israel are not being broken even though Israelites are being rejected for their unbelief and Gentiles are being saved through their faith in the Savior whom God has sent. Some Israelites are being saved. Israel's rejection is not complete; but "they are not all Israel, that are of Israel."

Or take an even more startling example of rejection. The two sons of Isaac, unlike Isaac and Ishmael, had the same mother as well as the same father; indeed they were twins. Yet before their birth and thus before they had "done anything good or bad" God rejected one and accepted the other as heir of the promises. He declared, "The elder shall serve the younger," and the whole course of history, as related to these sons and the nations which sprang from them, could be summed up in the words of the prophet Malachi, "Jacob I loved, but Esau I hated."

It is true that the "profane," faithless character of Esau justified God in rejecting him; nevertheless the action of God preceded his birth and was absolutely free and quite independent of any claims based upon birth or good works. It illustrates "the purpose of God according to election," showing that the choices of God, while always righteous and holy, are absolutely sovereign and not determined by human claims of birth or merit.

It also illustrates the fact that while the promises were made to Israel, God does not disregard his promises when he determines to accept some and to reject others from among those who are Israelites merely by natural descent.

Of course Paul does here bring to mind the mysteries of divine election and does intimate that the careers of Jacob and Esau were in some way determined before their birth; yet it is quite aside from the point to argue from these words that the eternal salvation or perdition of individual souls is determined by a divine decree "which has no relation to what they are or do."

The purpose of Paul is plain and practical. It is to warn any Israelite against supposing that simply because of his birth and his outward obedience to Jewish law he can claim from God a share in the promises made to Israel, and further, Paul thus definitely shows that God is faithful to his promises even when rejecting the present unbelieving masses of his chosen race.

That practical purpose of the apostle bears a message to men of all races today. No one should suppose that birth or blood gives one a right to the privileges of a child of God; one "must be born again." No one should allow his position in a Christian community or in a godly family to make him careless as to his personal relation to Christ. No one should claim that membership in a church or participation in the Sacraments can make him an heir to the glory of God; it is only by vital faith in Jesus Christ that we become Abraham's seed, and heirs according to promise.

## c. Israel's Rejection and God's Justice   Ch. 9:14-29

*14 What shall we say then? Is there unrighteousness with God? God forbid. 15 For he saith to Moses, I will have mercy on whom I have mercy, and I will have compassion on whom I have compassion. 16 So then it is not of him that willeth, nor of him that runneth, but of God that hath mercy. 17 For the scripture saith unto Pharaoh, For this very purpose did I raise thee up, that I might show in thee my power, and that my name might be published abroad in all the earth. 18 So then he hath mercy on whom he will, and whom he will he hardeneth.*

*19 Thou wilt say then unto me, Why doth he still find fault? For who withstandeth his will? 20 Nay but, O man, who art thou that repliest against God? Shall the thing formed say to him that formed it, Why didst thou make me thus? 21 Or hath not the potter a right over the clay, from the same lump to make one part a vessel unto honor, and another unto dishonor? 22 What if God, willing to show his wrath, and to make his power known, endured* with much longsuffering vessels of wrath fitted unto destruction: 23 and that he might make known the riches of his glory upon vessels of mercy, which he afore prepared unto glory, 24 even us, whom he also called, not from the Jews only, but also from the Gentiles? 25 As he saith also in Hosea,

> I will call that my people, which was not my people;
> And her beloved, that was not beloved.

26 And it shall be, that in the place where it was said unto them, Ye are not my people,

> There shall they be called sons of the living God.

27 And Isaiah crieth concerning Israel, If the number of the children of Israel be as the sand of the sea, it is the remnant that shall be saved: 28 for the Lord will execute his word upon the earth, finishing it and cutting it short. 29 And, as Isaiah hath said before,

> Except the Lord of Sabaoth had left us a seed,
> We had become as Sodom, and had been made like unto Gomorrah.

The hardening of Pharaoh's heart has proved a stubborn problem, if not an actual stumbling block to many readers of the Old Testament story. It has been supposed that God hardened Pharaoh's heart and then unjustly punished Pharaoh for his hardness.

However, it should be noted, first, that if God is said to have hardened Pharaoh's heart, it is said quite as distinctly that Pharaoh hardened his own heart. Secondly, God was working through natural laws, and the heart of Pharaoh was hardened as a result of his own free, defiant, and cruel choices and acts. Thirdly, it is evident that the story is not correctly interpreted if it is supposed to show injustice on the part of God, for Paul is here quoting the story with the one purpose of proving the justice of God. The very matter under discussion is that of divine justice. The question is just this: In saving certain Jews and many Gentiles, while most Jews are allowed to continue in unbelief, is not God exercising an unjust choice? On the contrary, Paul shows that according to Scripture, God himself asserts his freedom of choice in two similar or typical cases, namely, in showing mercy toward Moses and severity toward Pharaoh.

In the case of Moses it was not due to human will or effort, it was "not of him that willeth, nor of him that runneth," but it was due wholly to the sovereign grace of God that his great mercy was shown. So in the case of Pharaoh, it was the sovereign choice of God that selected him to be the historic example of God's resistless power and of his certainty to punish defiant and rebellious disobedience. Paul does not here mention the complementary truths of faith and fault on the part of men; he is asserting only the sovereign freedom of God, whether in showing mercy or in hardening, whether in the cases of Moses and Pharaoh, or in the case of the believing and unbelieving Jews in the days of Paul. The choices and actions of God are not capricious or unjust, but they are absolutely free and uncontrolled. (Vs. 14-18.)

If, however, God is sovereign and carries out his purposes through or in spite of the will of man, how can God blame men for disobedience or unbelief? Does not divine sovereignty abolish all human responsibility? Would not God be unjust if he punished those who rejected Christ?

Paul replies by another appeal to the Old Testament Scriptures. He cites the familiar parable of the potter. If the relation of God to men is that of the potter to the vessels he forms from the clay, how can man, the creature, find fault with the Creator? The potter has a right to make of the same clay one vessel for an honorable use, another for a dishonorable; can man, therefore, charge God with injustice if he chooses to show his severity toward those who merit his displeasure, and his mercy toward chosen objects of his grace?

Indeed, as creatures of God, men could hardly sit in judgment upon God and accuse him of injustice if he had been arbitrary and capricious and severe; but how can anyone accuse God of injustice in view of the way he actually has dealt with men?  He has been patient and long-suffering toward his impenitent people, Israel, and has purposed to show all the wealth of his glory toward the objects of his mercy, chosen not only from among the Jews, his covenant people, but even from among the Gentiles.  The sovereignty of God is absolute; yet it is never exercised in condemning men who ought to be saved, but rather, it has resulted in the salvation of men who deserved to be lost.  Surely no one can regard God as unjust if he is rejecting impenitent and unbelieving Israelites and is saving Gentiles who turn to him in penitence and faith. (Vs. 19-24.)

This salvation of Gentiles and rejection of Israel had indeed been predicted by the prophets, and thus, in further establishing the justice of God, Paul again appeals to Scripture.  In the case of the Gentiles he quotes the beautiful words of Hosea, spoken in reference to the apostate and idolatrous Ten Tribes but involving the same principle of divine pardon and mercy:

"I will call that my people, which was not my people;
And her beloved, that was not beloved."

And further, as these tribes were to be restored to their own land, so that the scene of their new adoption would be the same as that of their sin; thus the words spoken of them by Hosea are applied by Paul to Gentiles, who, in the lands where they had lived in ignorance of God or in disobedience to his will, would know the blessedness of being his children: "There shall they be called sons of the living God."

In the case of Israel, Paul quotes from Isaiah to show that it has been predicted that, for a time at least, the whole nation would be rejected and only a small remnant be saved.  Because of their unbelief, God would cut off his people, exercising his sharp and decisive sentence upon them, although in his mercy he would save some.  The prophet was probably describing the punishment of Israel in his own day, and the remnant which was to escape from the devastating hosts of Assyria; but Paul applies the words to those in Israel who at the time he was writing were being saved by the gospel message. So he applies, in a similar way, an earlier prediction of Isaiah to the effect that the whole apostate nation would be blotted out and forgotten were it not that the Lord of hosts, in his mercy, would save some to preserve their seed and name:

"Except the Lord of Sabaoth had left us a seed,
  We had become as Sodom, and had been made like unto Gomorrah."

From Sodom only four souls escaped; Gomorrah was utterly destroyed. Thus from the mouth of the Old Testament prophets Paul establishes the fact that God is not only just but merciful, even in his present rejection of Israel.   (Vs. 25-29.)

In the next paragraph (vs. 30-33) he shows that in this rejection, prophecy has merely passed into history: Gentiles are being saved while Israel as a nation is being set aside. The latter, however, is due to the fault of Israel. The paragraph properly belongs, therefore, to the next chapter, which deals with Israel's responsibility even as chapter nine has been setting forth God's sovereignty. It serves, however, as a climax to the present phase of the argument which is establishing God's justice. Even though he is acting in sovereign freedom, yet he is acting justly in setting aside a nation which is rejecting Christ, refusing God's way of salvation, and neglecting his offer of grace. The doctrines of election and divine sovereignty do perplex and baffle the mind of man; yet no little relief is found when one faces the complementary truths of human freedom and responsibility. Paul has not hesitated to speak boldly and without qualification in setting forth the sovereignty of God in the rejection of Israel; he will now speak with equal unreserve in revealing Israel's guilt, which after all is the occasion of Israel's rejection.

## 2. The Rejection of Israel Is Not Arbitrary
### Chs. 9:30 to 10:21

### a. *Israel's Failure to Accept Christ   Ch. 9:30-33*

> *30 What shall we say then?   That the Gentiles, who followed not after righteousness, attained to righteousness, even the righteousness which is of faith:   31 but Israel, following after a law of righteousness, did not arrive at that law.   32 Wherefore?   Because they sought it not by faith, but as it were by works.   They stumbled at the stone of stumbling; 33 even as it is written,*
>> *Behold, I lay in Zion a stone of stumbling and a rock of offence:*
>> *And he that believeth on him shall not be put to shame.*

It is a remarkable but familiar fact of religious history that men who most eagerly have sought to win for themselves the favor of God by fasts and forms and sacrifices and obedience to law have failed to secure either peace of conscience or victory over sin, while others, who long have been indifferent to religion and unmindful of God, by an act of simple faith, of surrender and trust, have obtained a sense of pardon and a consciousness of invincible moral power.   Many men today who think and talk the most about religion lack peace and purity and love, while others, comparatively ignorant of religious problems and processes, so abandon themselves to God that they enjoy his presence and find fulfilled in their lives all his promises of blessedness and grace.

This great fact Paul found illustrated on a national scale in the case of unbelieving Israel and the contrasted converts from among the Gentiles.   He is discussing in chapters nine, ten, and eleven, the problem of Israel's rejection; and as he passes to a new phase of his argument he practically restates the problem, but with an element which increases its perplexity.   He has been attempting to reconcile with the promises of God and the justice of God the fact that the chosen people are being lost while Gentiles are being saved. He now adds the consideration that the very people who are failing to attain salvation are earnestly seeking for salvation. "What shall we say then?" asks the apostle. What is the state of the case? What is the problem we are stating? It is this: Gentiles, not all but many Gentiles, "who followed not after righteousness," who did not make the attainment of righteousness their chief concern—these "attained to righteousness"; but Israel, as a nation, "following after a law of righteousness," seeking to obey the law which would win for them righteousness, "did not arrive at that law" but failed to attain what that law promised and enjoined.

"Wherefore?" asks Paul. "Because they sought it not by faith, but as it were by works." This is the explanation. This is the real answer to the problem. Israel is being rejected because of Israel's guilty and stubborn unbelief. There has been on the part of Israel no real submission to God, no actual abandonment to his will. Israel has been attempting to put God under obligation by formal observance of his law. Israel has failed because seeking for righteousness not by faith but by works. In the preceding portion of this chapter, Paul has viewed the problem of Israel's rejection in the light of God's sovereignty, which made it impossible for anyone to place God under obligation to save him; Paul now enters upon that portion of his discussion where he dwells upon Israel's responsibility, and shows that Israel's rejection is not arbitrary on the part of God but is due to Israel's unbelief. (Chs. 9:30 to 10:21.)

This unbelief has been given its supreme manifestation in Israel's rejection of the Messiah. Christ came as the One on whom Israel might have founded all its hopes of salvation, but he proved to be for Israel "a stone of stumbling and a rock of offence." If Israel has fallen, it is Israel's fault.

In referring to Christ, Paul does not at once name him,

but quotes and mingles two Old Testament prophecies in which God's appointed King, and even God himself, is designated as the hope of Israel but also as "a rock of offence" to those who showed themselves to him. Paul finds the fulfillment of the prophecies in Christ, and refers to him the blessed assurance that "he that believeth on him shall not be put to shame."

So Christ is presented to men today. The refusal to accept him as God's appointed Savior is to reveal the fact that one does not really wish to submit to the will of God. One who rests on him for righteousness, for salvation, for eternal life, will never be disappointed, will never "be put to shame"; but one who depends on his own goodness and righteousness, and therefore rejects Christ, condemns himself and finds Christ to be for him "a stone of stumbling and a rock of offence." The rejection or acceptance of Christ is still the proof of the attitude of a soul toward God, as being either guilty unbelief or saving faith.

### b. Israel's Refusal of God's Righteousness    Ch. 10:1-15

1 Brethren, my heart's desire and my supplication to God is for them, that they may be saved. 2 For I bear them witness that they have a zeal for God, but not according to knowledge. 3 For being ignorant of God's righteousness, and seeking to establish their own, they did not subject themselves to the righteousness of God. 4 For Christ is the end of the law unto righteousness to every one that believeth. 5 For Moses writeth that the man that doeth the righteousness which is of the law shall live thereby. 6 But the righteousness which is of faith saith thus, Say not in thy heart, Who shall ascend into heaven? (that is, to bring Christ down:) 7 or, Who shall descend into the abyss? (that is, to bring Christ up from the dead.) 8 But what saith it? The word is nigh thee, in thy mouth, and in thy heart: that is, the word of faith, which we preach: 9 because if thou shalt confess with thy mouth Jesus as Lord, and shalt believe in thy heart that God raised him from the dead, thou shalt be saved: 10 for with the heart man be-

*lieveth unto righteousness; and with the mouth confession is made unto salvation. 11 For the scripture saith, Whosoever believeth on him shall not be put to shame. 12 For there is no distinction between Jew and Greek: for the same Lord is Lord of all, and is rich unto all that call upon him: 13 for, Whosoever shall call upon the name of the Lord shall be saved. 14 How then shall they call on him in whom they have not believed? and how shall they believe in him whom they have not heard? and how shall they hear without a preacher? 15 and how shall they preach, except they be sent? even as it is written, How beautiful are the feet of them that bring glad tidings of good things!*

There would be no lack of converts to the Christian faith if all who profess to follow Christ felt for the spiritual welfare of their fellow countrymen the deep concern expressed by Paul for his own people: "Brethren, my heart's desire and my supplication to God is for them, that they may be saved."

This expression of deep solicitude for their salvation is due to the fact that he is about to emphasize even more severely his previous intimation that the rejection of Israel is due to the fault of the Israelites. His concern for them is deepened by the consideration that they really have a zeal for God and are making painful efforts to win his approval. Their zeal, however, is not according to true spiritual knowledge. They are seeking to attain a righteousness of their own and are thus refusing the righteousness which God provides.

Their own way of salvation, one indeed which men seem to prefer naturally, is by the way of strict observance of laws by which one achieves merit for himself. This way has come to its end in Christ. As a way of salvation it finds its termination in him; for everyone who has found peace and pardon through faith in him has abandoned the old way of seeking righteousness by works of the law.

That the old way was difficult, if not impossible, was implied by the lawgiver Moses when he wrote, "Ye shall therefore keep my statutes . . . ; which if a man do, he shall live in them"; by which he meant that life in all its fullness, here and hereafter, was to be attained by undeviating obedience to legal rules. Such an obedience, however, Paul earlier in this epistle has shown to be impossible.

We are not to conclude, however, that Moses deceived or mocked his people. In his day, and under his system, men could be right with God; but it was by the way of faith, which regarded the law as an expression of God's will and trusted in God for pardon and grace. Now that God has revealed himself more fully in Christ, true faith places no reliance upon the self-righteousness which consists in the formal observance of rules, but accepts the salvation, the power, the peace, the new life, which are offered in Christ.

In contrast with that old way of salvation, "the righteousness which is of faith" is supposed by Paul to speak and to say that it is near and accessible to all. It employs familiar words of Scripture to which it gives new meaning: There is no need to say who will go up to heaven to bring Christ down, or who will ascend into the deep to bring Christ from the dead, for the Christ who is the object of true faith is one who has already come to earth in the form of man, and has already been raised from the dead. The gospel message centers in such an incarnate and risen Christ. It is a message which is familiar to each one, "in thy mouth, and in thy heart."

The substance of the message is this: "Confess with your mouth Jesus as your Lord and believe in your heart that God has raised him from the dead and you shall be saved, for real faith of the heart results in righteousness and will naturally express itself in open confession." Paul refers here to incarnation and resurrection not as exclusive but as typical truths, as intimating a necessary belief in the divine person and saving work of Christ.

This way of salvation is now supported by a quotation from Scripture: "Whosoever believeth on him shall not be put to shame." The universal application of these words of Isaiah is warranted because no difference is made between Jews and Gentiles in the bestowal of righteousness upon believers, because the same Lord of all, even Jesus Christ, is rich in his bestowal of grace and salvation upon all who call upon him in faith and trust. That salvation is certain to be granted to all who so call upon Christ is shown by a quotation from Joel describing the deliverance to be granted in the Kingdom of the Messiah before the great day of the Lord.

A way of salvation so universal in its application demands a worldwide proclamation. This fact Paul emphasizes by a series of four significant questions: "How then shall they call on him in whom they have not believed? and how shall they believe in him whom they have not heard? and how shall they hear without a preacher? and how shall they preach, except they be sent?"

This universal character of the gospel has always been a valid and cogent argument for Christian missions. It should be noted, however, that in this passage the Lord is the one by whom the preachers are sent, and that those who hear the messengers really hear him in whose name they speak, and by hearing come to believe in him and to call upon him for salvation.

The glory of this mission is such that Paul describes it in words borrowed from Isaiah when depicting the messengers who carried the glad tidings of restoration from the captivity in Babylon. Thus indeed the messengers of Christ are carrying into all the world the good news of deliverance from sin and death, of a return to God, of the glorious Jerusalem above, of the joys of the ransomed, of the eternal blessings of the redeemed.

## c. Israel's Neglect of the Gospel Message   Ch. 10:16-21

16 But they did not all hearken to the glad tidings. For Isaiah saith, Lord, who hath believed our report? 17 So belief cometh of hearing, and hearing by the word of

*Christ.   18 But I say, Did they not hear?   Yea, verily,*
*Their sound went out into all the earth,*
*And their words unto the ends of the world.*
*19 But I say, Did Israel not know?   First Moses saith,*
*I will provoke you to jealousy with that which is no*
*nation,*
*With a nation void of understanding will I anger you.*
*20 And Isaiah is very bold, and saith,*
*I was found of them that sought me not;*
*I became manifest unto them that asked not of me.*
*21 But as to Israel he saith, All the day long did I spread*
*out my hands unto a disobedient and gainsaying people.*

Religious opportunities are too frequently neglected. Multitudes of men who are quite familiar with the gospel are indifferent to its message, while others who for the first time hear its glad tidings eagerly accept the salvation it offers in the name of Christ.   Of the former class were the Jews of Paul's day.   In proving that Israel's rejection is due to Israel's fault, Paul here shows that the people are without excuse, and that their rejection is due to their proud, stubborn, willful unbelief.

The "glad tidings of good things" were proclaimed to all, "but they did not all hearken"; far from it; Israel practically as a nation had rejected Christ.   This was the tragic fact; and this guilty unbelief had been predicted by Isaiah in his pathetic words, "Lord, who hath believed our report?"   The message had been sent and should have been received.   The opportunity for faith had been given, for "belief cometh of hearing, and hearing by the word of Christ."   That is, the gospel is not a matter of intuition or imagination or conjecture or reverie, but of revelation.   It is a message given by God to men; its sum and substance is the person and work of Christ; and faith consists in a humble, grateful acceptance of this message.

Israel could not plead as an excuse that this message had not been heard, for the gospel had been preached throughout the whole Roman world.   So wide was this proclamation that Paul quotes in reference to it the words of the psalmist written of the revelation of God in nature:

"Their sound went out into all the earth,
And their words unto the ends of the world."

As the silent voices of the skies proclaim to the whole world the power of the Creator, so the voices of Christian heralds are declaring in all lands the glory of the redeeming Christ.

Nor can the excuse be given that the gospel message has not been understood. That it was designed for other nations, and that Israel would be slow to accept it, had been predicted from the earliest days of Israel's history. Even Moses had declared that heathen would be given a share in the blessings of God's people and would thus excite the jealousy and anger of the Jews:

"I will provoke you to jealousy with that which is no nation,
With a nation void of understanding will I anger you."

The words were in the ancient days a warning to the idolatrous people of Israel. If they continued to be untrue to Jehovah, he would provoke their jealousy by showing mercy to nations who were, from the Jewish point of view, no real nations, and void of religious knowledge. Such a situation was paralleled in Paul's day by the rejection of Israel and the call of the Gentiles.

The same truth was set forth boldly by Isaiah, in spite of the natural displeasure of his people at such a prediction. Words which referred first of all to apostate Jews are applied in principle to Gentiles:

"I was found of them that sought me not;
I became manifest unto them that asked not of me."

Finally Paul makes another quotation from the prophet to show that God's love had been unique and exhaustless. He had ever sought to bring Israel back into fellowship with himself. He had stood with outstretched hands. He had called them to him by the voices of pleading messengers. Last of all he had sent his Son. If Israel was still unsaved—if, for the time, the nation was rejected—it was only because of Israel's fault. The people of Israel were disobedient and rebellious. In truth God could say to them, "All the day long did I spread out my hands unto a disobedient and gainsaying people."

How tenderly God is dealing today with many who are refusing his gospel! Patiently he is pleading; his offers are full of grace and mercy. Where will the fault lie in the case of those who reject his messages of love?

### 3. THE REJECTION OF ISRAEL IS NOT FINAL
#### Ch. 11

*a. The Present Election of Grace   Ch. 11:1-10*

*1 I say then, Did God cast off his people? God forbid. For I also am an Israelite, of the seed of Abraham, of the tribe of Benjamin. 2 God did not cast off his people which he foreknew. Or know ye not what the scripture saith of Elijah? how he pleadeth with God against Israel: 3 Lord, they have killed thy prophets, they have digged down thine altars; and I am left alone, and they seek my life. 4 But what saith the answer of God unto him? I have left for myself seven thousand men, who have not bowed the knee to Baal. 5 Even so then at this present time also there is a remnant according to the election of grace. 6 But if it is by grace, it is no more of works: otherwise grace is no more grace. 7 What then? That which Israel seeketh for, that he obtained not; but the election obtained it, and the rest were hardened: 8 according as it is written, God gave them a spirit of stupor, eyes that they should not see, and ears that they should not hear, unto this very day. 9 And David saith,*

*Let their table be made a snare, and a trap,*
*And a stumblingblock, and a recompense unto them:*
*10 Let their eyes be darkened, that they may not see,*
*And bow thou down their back always.*

Can Jews be converted to faith in Christ? Is Jewish evangelization a futile and impertinent enterprise on the part of the Christian church? Is the spiritual condition of Israel hopeless? To these important and searching questions of the present day, Paul here gives his inspired reply.

It is not difficult to trace the train of thought which has given rise to these questions. Paul has been discussing the problem of Israel's rejection; that is, he has been attempting to reconcile the Old Testament predictions of Israel's godliness and glory with Israel's present failure to share in the salvation which the Messiah is bringing to Gentile believers. The ninth chapter of the epistle has shown that Israel's present rejection is not inconsistent with the inspired prediction or with the justice of God; chapter ten has shown that Israel's rejection is due to Israel's stubborn unbelief; chapter eleven reveals that Israel's rejection is neither complete (vs. 1-10) nor final (vs. 11-32), but is to issue in such a national restoration as will result in universal blessing. Paul closes the discussion with adoration and praise. (Vs. 33-36.)

Chapter nine has emphasized God's sovereignty; chapter ten, Israel's sin; chapter eleven declares that according to the providence of God even Israel's sin is to be overruled to further the redemption of the whole world.

"I say then, Did God cast off his people?" One might have so concluded from the solemn arraignment of rebellious and unbelieving Israel with which the previous chapter had closed. "God forbid," cries the apostle, and he at once explains why he rejects with horror the very idea as impious and incredible. "I also am an Israelite, of the seed of Abraham, of the tribe of Benjamin." He is himself a Jew by birth and not a proselyte, a lineal descendant of Abraham, and a member of the tribe which, with Judah, formed the restored nation after the exile and became the hope of the world. No wonder that he so vehemently denies that God has repudiated his people!

"God did not cast off his people which he foreknew." It is true that the case of Israel seems desperate, but the situation is exactly like that which existed in the days of Elijah. The poor, disheartened prophet had stood on the slopes of lonely Horeb and had cried out in despair, "The children of Israel have forsaken thy covenant, thrown down thine altars, and slain thy prophets with the sword; and I, even I only, am left; and they seek my life, to take it away," but God had made answer, "Yet will I leave me seven thousand in Israel, . . . which have not bowed unto Baal." Thus Paul concludes, "Even so then at this present time also there is a remnant according to the election of grace."

It was not due to their merit or their own attainments that such a saved remnant existed; it was due wholly to the grace of God. Yet it did exist. Jewish converts formed a very considerable fraction of the church at Rome, and a larger fraction still of the church throughout the world.

No Jewish convert today must allow himself to be overwhelmed by his loneliness; nor must the church look upon the conversion of Jews as an impossible task. In proportion to the efforts made, more converts are being secured from among the Jews than from among any other race. Nor should we feel discouraged in any work to which God has called us. When doubt and denial seem universal and the cause of the church appears desperate, let no prophet of God take too gloomy a view of the situation; let no one take himself too seriously and suppose that he is the only soul loyal to the Lord. There are always the seven thousand faithful ones, always "a remnant according to the election of grace," always a church within the church through which God is working for the redemption of the world.

On the other hand, it cannot be denied that the Jews as a nation are stubbornly fixed in their unbelief. "What then?" writes the apostle. Although this remnant does exist, what are we to say about the people as a whole? We cannot but admit the fact that "that which Israel seeketh for, that he obtained not; but the election obtained it, and the rest were hardened." This, too, is in accordance with the predictions of the prophet. He declared that the people of Israel failed to receive the very righteousness they sought and that because of their sin and unbelief they were judicially hardened so that they could not believe: "God gave them a spirit of stupor, eyes that they should not see, and ears that they should not hear, unto this very day." Or, as the psalmist declared, "Let their table be made a snare," that is, let the place in which they feel secure, or the very objects in which they delight, prove to be the source of their downfall and the occasion of their ruin.

Paul recognized the noble but misguided efforts of the Jews to attain righteousness and to win the favor of God. The law in which they delighted proved to be their "snare," their "trap," their "stumblingblock"; because of false confidence in their ability to keep its precepts and their stubborn rejection of Christ, it became their "recompense," that is to say, their perverse attitude toward the gospel reacted in an incapacity to understand and to receive it. In consequence they were in spiritual blindness and bondage, groping for light and bending beneath burdens too heavy to be borne.

Such is the pathetic picture of many serious men today. They earnestly seek to live right lives, but trusting to their own strength and righteousness they reject the grace that is offered in Christ; they refuse to accept the pardon and peace and power which he is ready to give. They stumble along in darkness, they struggle in weakness and weariness, when in him they might find rest for their souls.

## b. The Future Salvation of Israel   Ch. 11:11-32

*11 I say then, Did they stumble that they might fall? God forbid: but by their fall salvation is come unto the Gentiles, to provoke them to jealousy. 12 Now if their fall is the riches of the world, and their loss the riches of the Gentiles; how much more their fullness? 13 But I speak to you that are Gentiles. Inasmuch then as I am an apostle of Gentiles, I glorify my ministry; 14 if by any means I may provoke to jealousy them that are my flesh, and may save some of them. 15 For if the casting away of them is the reconciling of the world, what shall the receiving of them be, but life from the dead? 16 And if the firstfruit is holy, so is the lump: and if the root is holy, so are the branches. 17 But if some of the branches were broken off, and thou, being a wild olive, wast grafted in among them, and didst become partaker with them of the root of the fatness of the olive tree; 18 glory not over the branches: but if thou gloriest, it is not thou that bearest the root, but the root thee. 19 Thou wilt say then, Branches were broken off, that I might be grafted in. 20 Well; by their unbelief they were broken off, and thou standest by thy faith. Be not high-minded, but fear: 21 for if God spared not the natural branches, neither will he spare thee. 22 Behold then the goodness and severity of God: toward them that fell, severity; but toward thee, God's goodness, if thou continue in his goodness: otherwise thou also shalt be cut off. 23 And they also, if they continue not in their unbelief, shall be grafted in: for God is able to graft them in again. 24 For if thou wast cut out of that which is by nature a wild olive tree, and wast grafted contrary to nature into a good olive tree; how much more shall these, which are the natural* branches, *be grafted into their own olive tree?*

*25 For I would not, brethren, have you ignorant of this mystery, lest ye be wise in your own conceits, that a hardening in part hath befallen Israel, until the fulness of the Gentiles be come in; 26 and so all Israel shall be saved: even as it is written,*

*There shall come out of Zion the Deliverer;*
*He shall turn away ungodliness from Jacob:*
*27 And this is my covenant unto them,*
*When I shall take away their sins.*
*28 As touching the gospel, they are enemies for your sake: but as touching the election, they are beloved for the fathers' sake. 29 For the gifts and the calling of God are not repented of. 30 For as ye in time past were disobedient to God, but now have obtained mercy by their disobedience, 31 even so have these also now been disobedient,*

*that by the mercy shown to you they also may now obtain mercy.  32 For God hath shut up all unto disobedience, that he might have mercy upon all.*

What is to be the future of the Jewish people?   By intermarriage and by the abandonment of distinguishing customs are they to be amalgamated and lost among the other races of the world?   Or, as is now true of many, are they to lose their ancestral faith and, as a people possessing great elements of power and yet lacking moral restraint, are they to become a menace to civilization?   Or again, is the dream of Zionism to be realized, is a Jewish state to be established in Palestine, is the nation to be reborn, and is it to add another problem and peril to the international politics of the world?   Far different from any of these alternatives is the prediction of the apostle Paul.   He asserts that the present rejection of Israel is being overruled for the salvation of Gentiles; that the latter should be warned against unbelief by the present condition of Israel, and also warned against pride in view of the future restoration of Israel which is to result in the spiritual renewal of the whole human race.

The providential purpose served by the present unbelief of Israel is twofold: first, the rejection of the gospel by the Jews has resulted in the preaching of the gospel to the Gentiles; and secondly, spiritual blessings thus brought to the Gentiles will ultimately stir the Jews to emulation, will result in their conversation, and will issue in universal blessing.

"I say then, Did they stumble that they might fall?" Is the condition of Israel incurable?   Is their repudiation final?   Is their ruin complete?   "God forbid," writes the apostle, "but by their fall salvation is come unto the Gentiles," and this is in order to arouse unbelieving Israel to emulation and so to bring them back to the place which rightfully belongs to them.

"Therefore," continues the apostle, "if the fall of Israel

has brought to the world a wealth of spiritual blessing, by giving the gospel to the world and if their defection has thus enriched the world, what will result when they all are brought to Christ?" Or, as one has paraphrased the sentence, "If the Gentiles have been enriched in a sense through the very miscarriage and disaster of Israel, what wealth is in store for them in the great return, when all Israel shall be saved—when God hath made the pile complete!"

Why the future of the Jew is of such deep concern to Paul, the apostle of the Gentiles, he now explains. It is because his mission to the Gentiles is vitally related to his own countrymen. The more successful he can make his mission, the more faithfully he can discharge it, the greater will be the certainty that some Jews will be stirred to jealousy and be saved, and all who are saved go to make up that promised "fulness" of the Jews which will result in universal blessing. "For if the casting away" of the Jews, continues the apostle, has been the means of reconciling the world to God, by diverting the gospel to the Gentiles, in what will the restoration of Israel result but in a spiritual revival for all mankind, in a veritable "life from the dead?"

That there is to be such a national restoration of the Jews, Paul argues from their actual relationship to God. He employs two figures of speech. The "firstfruit" which is offered to God makes holy the entire mass from which it is taken; it indicates that the whole belongs to God. So, too, the root of a tree gives life and character to the branches, and "if the root is holy, so are the branches." (Vs. 11-16.)

Thus it is with Israel. The ancient patriarchs from which the race sprang belonged to God; they were chosen of him, and therefore the people which came from them were holy; they are the people of God, and in spite of temporary unbelief and rejection, they will yet appear in their real character and will manifest that relation to God which is theirs by right, and is in accordance with his changeless purpose.

Is there not in all this a message of cheer and comfort for all those who have been "sanctified in Christ Jesus" and "called to be saints"? Does not God show himself able to overrule for good even their failures and their faults, and when in penitence they are brought back to him, does he not use them in enlarging spheres of service, and make them of wider blessing to the world?

Paul's reference to the Jewish race as branches from a holy root might be employed by Gentile Christians as an argument to disprove the predicted restoration of Israel and as a ground for their own self-confidence, because the casting away of the Jews and the creation of a Gentile church might indicate that this new people of God had permanently displaced rejected Israel.

This is a very common misconception among Christians today. They disregard as visionary all predictions concerning the national future of Israel, and they appropriate to themselves all the blessings promised to the ancient people of God.

All this Paul anticipates; and from the simile of the root and the branches he draws two special lessons: one of humility, for Gentile believers; another of hope, for Israel.

The people of God, as forming one continuous body, according to a figure taken from the prophecy of Jeremiah, are pictured as "a green olive-tree, fair with goodly fruit." The root, or stock, from which Jews and Gentiles all receive their spiritual strength and nourishment is found in the patriarchs and other believers from whom the people of God have sprung. The branches are the individuals who derive their life from the body to which they belong. These branches are of two kinds: first, the original branches representing the Jews, some of which have been "cut off" because of unbelief; and second, branches from a wild olive, which have been grafted in, representing the Gentile church. Such grafting, Paul insists, is a wholly unnatural process. Shoots from a wild tree are never grafted into a cultivated stock; only the reverse process would produce good fruit. Paul has been accused of ignorance of horticulture because of his suggesting such grafting as is "contrary to nature"; but that is the very point of his argument. Gentile Christians are reminded that any virtues or blessings that they possess are due wholly to the grace of God and not to any merit of their own. These favors have been received through faith and, at best, Gentile believers only share a life drawn from a Jewish root. If Jewish branches "were broken off" that Gentile believers might be grafted in, this is no reason for pride and self-confidence on the part of these Gentiles. On the contrary, they should be warned, by the breaking off of the Jewish branches, of the peril of unbelief. At any time they themselves may be cut off; it would be a much less violent process to break off the wild olive branches than it was to break off those which belonged originally to the cultivated tree. The Gentile Christians, therefore, should observe and take to heart the goodness of God shown toward themselves and the severity of God shown toward Israel, and they should be warned that such goodness can be enjoyed only by those who continue in faith, loyal to God and dependent upon his will.

On the other hand, the second lesson is still more impressive, the lesson of hope for Israel. If the bringing of Gentiles into fellowship with the people of God was as unnatural as the grafting of wild olive branches into a cultivated stock, much more easily will God be able to restore to their original place these Jewish branches and to graft them into "their own olive tree." (Vs. 16-24.)

Such lessons are greatly needed today. What could be more unworthy or more unreasonable than for Gentile Christians to despise unbelieving Jews? Christians have merely inherited the blessings which through Jews have been brought to the whole world. The words of Christ, "Salvation is from the Jews," should never be forgotten.

Nor must Gentile believers be skeptical about the conversion of Israel. The surprising thing is not that Jews can be brought back into the body of God's true people; they have every spiritual and religious advantage. The strange thing is that Gentiles can be saved in spite of their inheritance of pantheism and atheism and idolatry. The conversion of a heathen may be regarded as a marvel. What is more natural on the part of a Jew than his return to the real faith of his fathers and his acceptance of the Messiah predicted by his prophets, of the Redeemer who came first of all to save his own people?

Paul now distinctly predicts the conversion of Israel. He indicates the importance of the event by using, to introduce his prediction, a characteristic phrase which he frequently employs for this purpose: "I would not, brethren, have you ignorant." He indicates further that this event has been divinely disclosed to him, for he describes it as a "mystery," by which Paul always means a secret once hidden but now revealed. Still further he states his desire to have the Roman church know of this coming conversion of Israel, lest this church might be wise in its own conceits and might imagine that it was to retain permanently the religious supremacy of the world.

How strangely the Roman church still labors under that delusion, and how surprisingly Protestants imitate Rome in their appraisal of the Jew! The fact is, as Paul declares, that the unbelief of Israel is only partial: "a hardening in part hath befallen Israel"; it is only temporary: "until the fulness of the Gentiles be come in," that is, until the "full complement of the Gentiles," or the Gentile nations as a whole, are converted or brought into the Christian church; and so, in consequence, all Israel shall be saved.

Evidently Paul is speaking here of Israel as a nation; he is not referring to every individual Israelite; just as in speaking of the "fulness of the Gentiles" he does not mean to indicate every individual in the Gentile world. Nor yet does he refer to the dead; nor to those who are to die before this salvation of Israel comes to pass. Paul is speaking here of nations and he is pointing to a time when Gentile kingdoms and the people of Israel shall be united in the blessings of a redeemed world.

Paul confirms his prediction by a quotation from Isaiah, in which it is stated that a Deliverer "shall come out of Zion" who "shall turn away ungodliness from Jacob," who will secure for Israel the benefits of a new covenant of grace and of forgiveness. Whether the reference here is to the first or the second coming of the Messiah is not made plain. The hope of Israel is in Christ, who surely has come and is now giving deliverance from sin to all who put their trust in him.

If Israel now especially seems to need such a deliverance, this should only make one more certain that the prophecy will be fulfilled, for in the divine plan, according to which the good tidings of salvation have been preached, the Jews in their unbelief have been treated as enemies of God in order that Gentiles might be saved; but this does not alter the fact that the people of Israel are the chosen people of God, and "beloved for the fathers' sake." God has given them special blessings, he has called them to a high destiny, and he never revokes his choice. That there is a parallel in the case of the Gentile church to the case of Israel, Paul further points out, and it is mentioned as a ground of universal hope. It was through Israel's disobedience and rejection of the gospel that the mercy of God came to the Roman believers; even so, the mercy now shown to Gentile believers will be the occasion of Israel's repentance and of Israel's enjoyment of divine favor. In both cases God's universal plan and purpose of salvation is being carried out. God, so to speak, has locked up in the prison house of hopeless unbelief and sin all mankind, both Jews and Gentiles, that he might show toward all in their absolute hopelessness his free and unmerited grace. This does not mean that Jews and Gentiles are not re-

sponsible for the unbelief and sin which resulted in their
helplessness and hopelessness; nor does it mean that ultimately every individual will be saved; nor yet that any
individual is saved without faith.   These truths are elsewhere safeguarded.   Paul is here reaching the great climax
of his epistle and is affirming not only that Israel is yet
to be saved in spite of present unbelief and rejection but
also that ultimately all nations are to be included in the
blessings which by his mercy and grace God is providing
through Jesus Christ our Lord.   (Vs. 25-32.)

### c. The Doxology   Ch. 11:33-36

> 33 O the depth of the riches both of the wisdom and
> the knowledge of God! how unsearchable are his judg-
> ments, and his ways past tracing out! 34 For who hath
> known the mind of the Lord? or who hath been his coun-
> sellor? 35 or who hath first given to him, and it shall be
> recompensed unto him again? 36 For of him, and through
> him, and unto him, are all things. To him be the glory
> for ever. Amen.

The doxologies which occur not infrequently in the
Pauline epistles are stately, majestic, sublime, and yet ap-
parently quite spontaneous.   They seem to arise naturally
from the emotions of a heart stirred by the contemplation
of the matchless grace and goodness of God.   Thus when
the apostle has clearly set forth the way of salvation which
God has prepared in Jesus Christ for all mankind, when
he has shown that men are justified freely, that the rejection is due to the fault of Israel, that this rejection has been
overruled for the salvation of Gentiles and ultimately will
give place to a national restoration which will result in
universal blessing, no wonder that the survey of such a
vast panorama of divine providence is succeeded by a
hymn of praise to "the depth of the riches both of the wisdom and the knowledge of God!"

Possibly it is best to regard these great words as coordinate and to read, as in the margin, "O the depth of the riches and the wisdom and the knowledge of God!" The riches of God would thus refer to "the wealth of love that enables God to meet, and far more than meet, the appalling necessities of the world."

In any case, "the wisdom and the knowledge" which Paul adores refer to God's comprehensive view of all things and his penetrating perception of details, which enable him to adapt his love to all the forces and conditions of the world, even to failure and unbelief and sin, and to work out his plans and purposes of grace.

His "judgments," whether of punishment or of salvation, are "unsearchable"; his "ways" of dealing with men are "past tracing out." This is the reason for worship; this is the occasion for faith. We know only in part. However, if in one case, as in that of Israel, his mysterious providence has been vindicated, therefore in other cases, we can await his explanations and the ultimate demonstration of his love.

Surely God's ways are "past tracing out," for, to quote from the Old Testament, no one has been his "counsellor" so as to know how he would proceed to attain his purposes, and so rich is he that he needs nothing at the hands of man; all that he gives must be the expression of grace, as none can merit anything from him; and this is true because in this vast universe, and specifically in the sphere of salvation, all things have their source in him, through him they flow as he upholds, rules, and directs; he is their final cause, their exalted goal; they serve his eternal purpose, his gracious ends. Therefore, "to him be the glory for ever."

This is the expression of a faith which trusts where it cannot understand, which loves when it cannot explain, which reasons wisely that nothing but good can ultimately come from God to those who accept the grace he has revealed in the gift of his Son, our Savior and our Lord.

# III
# PRACTICAL EXHORTATIONS

Chs. 12:1 to 15:13

## A. AS MEMBERS OF THE CHURCH   Ch. 12

### 1. THE APPEAL TO CONSECRATION   Ch. 12:1-2

*1 I beseech you therefore, brethren, by the mercies of
God, to present your bodies a living sacrifice, holy, acceptable to God, which is your spiritual service. 2 And
be not fashioned according to this world: but be ye transformed by the renewing of your mind, that ye may prove
what is the good and acceptable and perfect will of God.*

Paul always bases duty upon doctrine; he traces life to
belief; he shows that character is determined by creed.
Therefore, when in twelve chapters of his epistle he has
set forth in logical fashion the great doctrines of the Christian faith, he proceeds to give a series of practical exhortations which indicate how Christian believers ought to live.
These exhortations are in large measure summarized by a
comprehensive appeal to consecration. (Vs. 1-2.) This
appeal is linked to the preceding portion of the epistle by
a logical and significant connective, "therefore." "I beseech you therefore, brethren, by the mercies of God,"
writes the apostle. These "mercies of God" point back to
the statements that Christians have been justified by faith
in Christ the Son, that they are being sanctified by the
power of the Holy Spirit, and that they are to be glorified
as heirs of God the Father. In view of such mercies comes
the appeal to consecration. This is the real logic of Christianity. We do not serve God to win his favor but because
we have received his favor we serve him in gratitude and
love.

This appeal to consecration is twofold. It is described as an act and an activity, as a crisis and a process, as a gift and a life.

The act is pictured, in figures drawn from the Old Testament ritual, as a "sacrifice" (v. 1). Our bodies, and thus, too, our souls of which our bodies are agents and instruments, are to be offered to God once for all in a definite act of self-dedication. This sacrifice is described as "living," in contrast with the ancient sacrifices the life of which was taken before the offering was placed upon the altar; in fact, our bodies and spirits are to be animated by the new life which comes from faith in Christ. This sacrifice is "holy," that is, "consecrated," separated from sin, and separated unto the service of God. It is certain to be "acceptable to God," like the rising in his presence of a "sweet savor" offering of old. Such a sacrifice is further described as a supreme form of religious service; it is "spiritual" in contrast with offerings which were merely material and physical; it is a "service," that is, a cult or priestly ritual; in fact, such an act of consecration forms the most sublime of liturgies.

This act, however, must be followed by an activity. This gift of self must issue in a life of service, this dedication of the body must result in a transformation of character and in doing the will of God. (V. 2.)

This new activity is described both negatively and positively. One so consecrated to God must not be "fashioned according to this world." The phrase "this world," or "age," pictures the sphere or form of life from which God is excluded, the spirit of which is selfishness, the prince of which is Satan. One who belongs to God must not be controlled by worldly precepts, by selfish motives, by sinful impulses. On the other hand, he must be "transformed" by accepting the will of Christ as the controlling principle of his life and by allowing the continual indwelling of the Spirit of Christ as the dominating power of his life. His character and conduct will not be determined by a mere imitation of Christ, but by the transforming energy of a divine, indwelling presence, irradiating his whole being. The supreme purpose of such a moral and spiritual transfiguration is that one may "prove," or find out by practical personal experience, what the will of God is, that is, what is in itself "good," what is "acceptable" to God, what is ethically complete and "perfect."

Such a blessed experience, issuing from a true consecration of self, should be enjoyed by everyone who has known the power of the gospel and has accepted the manifold mercies of God.

## 2. THE EXERCISE OF GIFTS   Ch. 12:3-8

*3 For I say, through the grace that was given me, to every man that is among you, not to think of himself more highly than he ought to think; but so to think as to think soberly, according as God hath dealt to each man a measure of faith. 4 For even as we have many members in one body, and all the members have not the same office: 5 so we, who are many, are one body in Christ, and severally members one of another. 6 And having gifts differing according to the grace that was given to us, whether prophecy, let us prophesy according to the proportion of our faith; 7 or ministry, let us give ourselves to our ministry; or he that teacheth, to his teaching; 8 or he that exhorteth, to his exhorting: he that giveth, let him do it with liberality; he that ruleth, with diligence; he that showeth mercy, with cheerfulness.*

Having made his comprehensive appeal for consecration of life, the apostle proceeds to indicate more in particular the duties which devolve upon Christians, and first of all he enjoins those which belong to them as members of the church. He begins with an exhortation to humility in exercising the different gifts and opportunities for service which are granted to believers. He intimates that such humility will be a natural result of true dedication to God. Such may be the force of the word "for" with which the exhortation opens; since if we have given ourselves wholly to God, and if all our talents and gifts for service are entrusted to us by him, we may be expected to have a humble opinion of ourselves.

Paul was himself an example of such humility as he gave this very advice, since he indicated that he did so "through the grace that was given" him. His authority as a teacher, his opportunity for advising his readers, were thus assigned by him to the goodness and grace of God, leaving no occasion of self-exaltation or pride.

To a similarly humble judgment of himself each member of the church is exhorted; he is urged "not to think of himself more highly than he ought to think; but so to think as to think soberly"; and surely each one needs such an exhortation, for to himself each one is naturally the most important person in the world, and it is difficult to regard others with a due sense of moral proportion. Whatever differences exist must be due to a divine provision, "according as God hath dealt to each man a measure of faith." Thus, whatever estimates we place upon ourselves, all must be controlled by the humility which is inspired when we remember that we belong to God and that whatever we are and possess comes from him.

A further safeguard against pride is found in the fact that in the Christian church there is a wide variety of gifts; no one should expect to possess all the talents and to do all the work necessary for the life of the church. As in the human body there are many members, each with its special function, so all believers, because of their common relation to Christ, form one body in which each member has a definite place to fill and a special work to do. The gifts which are granted to the several members are to be exercised not with a view to securing praise or for gratifying vanity but for the benefit of the whole body.

If one possesses the gift of prophecy, by which is meant not so much the ability to predict as the power of unfolding and preaching the revealed will of God, he should exercise this gift not in proud self-confidence or with vain endeavor to be original but within the limits of his own belief and in accordance with the faith God has granted him.

One may have a special gift for ministering to the needs of his fellow Christians; another may have a gift for teaching spiritual truth; still another may find that his gift lies in the ability to speak words of wisdom and comfort.

To one, God gives a spirit of liberality, or of sincere unselfishness which fits him for the work of supplying relief to those who are in need. To another is given the grace of diligence, or moral earnestness, to equip him for his sphere of leadership in the church; to another is granted a spirit of cheerfulness, of joyfulness and sunny brightness, which qualifies him to visit the sick and the poor and the sorrowing.

However, each talent is to be applied, each gift is to be exercised, with a humble regard to the limits of one's own appointed task and with a desire to benefit others, for whose common good each gift is allotted and each talent is designed.

### 3. THE MANIFESTATION OF LOVE　Ch. 12:9-21

*9 Let love be without hypocrisy. Abhor that which is evil; cleave to that which is good. 10 In love of the brethren be tenderly affectioned one to another; in honor preferring one another; 11 in diligence not slothful; fervent in spirit; serving the Lord; 12 rejoicing in hope; patient in tribulation; continuing stedfastly in prayer; 13 communicating to the necessities of the saints, given to hospitality. 14 Bless them that persecute you; bless, and curse not. 15 Rejoice with them that rejoice; weep with them that weep. 16 Be of the same mind one toward another. Set not your mind on high things, but condescend to things that are lowly. Be not wise in your own conceits. 17 Render to no man evil for evil. Take thought for things honorable in the sight of all men. 18 If it be possible, as*

*much as in you lieth, be at peace with all men. 19 Avenge
not yourselves, beloved, but give place unto the wrath of
God: for it is written, Vengeance belongeth unto me; I will
recompense, saith the Lord. 20 But if thine enemy hun-
ger, feed him; if he thirst, give him to drink: for in so doing thou shalt heap coals of fire upon his head. 21 Be
not overcome of evil, but overcome evil with good.*

Having urged upon his readers the need of humility in
the exercise of their various gifts, Paul next exhorts them
to manifest love toward all their fellow members in the
church of Christ. It is true, the paragraph contains many
related maxims for Christian living, but love seems to be
the ruling thought. Thus humility, "the most beautiful
flower in the Christian garden," is linked here with charity,
"which is the bond of perfectness." This love must be
"without hypocrisy," unfeigned, neither hiding what one
is nor pretending to be what one is not; and it must not
countenance moral weakness or allow mutual indulgence;
it should make one shrink in horror from "that which is
evil" and hold with determination to "that which is good."

In the matter of love for fellow Christians, as toward
brethren in the one family of God, there must be not only
moral purity but also warm affection, with a real eagerness
to show honor each to the other. Zeal in Christian service
must not be allowed to flag. The "spiritual glow" must be
maintained. The absorbing aim of life must be to serve
the Lord Christ. The hope of future blessedness should
be a source of joy even in the midst of severe persecutions, which indeed must be endured with patience. Continual prayer, maintained with consistency and effort, will
make such patience possible. Love must be shown further by sharing one's goods with needy Christians, and by
making a practice of showing hospitality.

While such charity is to mark our attitude toward our
fellow Christians, we are to show the same disposition
toward all men. We must bless and not curse our perse-
cutors. We must be sympathetic, quite as ready to rejoice

with those who rejoice as we are to do the thing which is quite as easy, namely, to "weep with them that weep."

We must maintain a loving harmony with one another. Instead of cherishing selfish ambitions, we must give ourselves over to humble tasks. We must not be self-conceited.

Even to our enemies we are not to repay evil for evil. We are so to live as not to provoke enmity, so to live that our conduct may commend itself as honorable to men; if possible, we are to live at peace with all men, at any rate so far as concerns our own part.

Even when wronged we are not to take revenge, but are to let the wrath of God have its way. He will right our wrongs; for we have the promise, "Vengeance, belongeth unto me; I will recompense, saith the Lord."

On the contrary, as contrasted either with taking revenge or resigning the case to the judgment of God, we must do as the Scripture bids (Prov. 25:21-22):

"If thine enemy be hungry, give him bread to eat;
   And if he be thirsty, give him water to drink:
   For thou wilt heap coals of fire upon his head";

by which is meant, "You will make him feel that burning sense of shame and remorse which comes to one whose unkindness is repaid by love." In a word, do not let the evil done to you drive you to revenge, but overcome evil by the good you do to your adversary, transforming him from an enemy into a friend.

## B. AS CITIZENS OF THE STATE   Ch. 13

### 1. CIVIL DUTIES   Ch. 13:1-7

*1 Let every soul be in subjection to the higher powers: for there is no power but of God; and the* powers *that be are ordained of God. 2 Therefore he that resisteth the power, withstandeth the ordinance of God: and they that withstand shall receive to themselves judgment. 3 For*

*rulers are not a terror to the good work, but to the evil.
And wouldest thou have no fear of the power? do that
which is good, and thou shalt have praise from the same:
4 for he is a minister of God to thee for good. But if thou
do that which is evil, be afraid; for he beareth not the sword
in vain: for he is a minister of God, an avenger for wrath
to him that doeth evil. 5 Wherefore ye must needs be in
subjection, not only because of the wrath, but also for
conscience' sake. 6 For for this cause ye pay tribute also;
for they are ministers of God's service, attending continually upon this very thing. 7 Render to all their dues:
tribute to whom tribute is due; custom to whom custom;
fear to whom fear; honor to whom honor.*

In the preceding chapter Paul has been pointing out to
Christians their duty of showing humility and love as members of the church; here he enforces the duty of loyalty as
citizens of the state. The church and the state occupy
different spheres, according to the apostle, yet both are
divine institutions. All attempts to combine the functions
of church and state lead to serious confusion. However,
because he is a member of the church, a Christian is not
free from his duties to the state, but rather is under obligation to perform these duties with the greater faithfulness.

What local conditions may have led Paul to discuss the
question of Christian citizenship is largely a matter of conjecture. Yet evidently it was necessary that the church in
the Roman capital should not be misled by any false ideas
as to the nature of the Kingdom of God, that it should not
be allied with any movements which tended toward anarchy, insurrection, or rebellion. All Christians need to
have a definite understanding of their right relation to the
state, and to accept sound principles of Christian politics.
These principles were all included in the comprehensive
rule of the Master: "Render unto Cæsar the things that are
Cæsar's, and unto God the things that are God's." Here
Paul expands this rule in more detail and with more fullness than elsewhere in his writings, yet with marked so-

briety, wisdom, and restraint.

"Let every soul be in subjection to the higher powers," writes the apostle. The duty of submission to civil authorities is thus without exception, no matter how high or privileged one's social position may be, no matter what political theories one may hold, no matter what religious views one may profess.

The reason for such individual and universal submission is found in the fact that civil government has its source in God: "The powers that be are ordained of God." Therefore to resist the authorized officers of the government is to resist God, for they are his rightful representatives; and such resistance will receive condemnation, by human authorities and by divine sanction, for "they that withstand shall receive to themselves judgment."

Another reason for submission to civil authorities is the beneficent aim of human government, "for rulers are not a terror to the good work, but to the evil." Therefore one who conducts himself rightly need have no fear of civil officials, but one who is lawless in his behavior may well stand in dread, for "the sword" as the symbol of power to punish, is not given to a ruler "in vain." The ruler will inflict penalties when they are demanded and he will do so as an administrator of divine justice, "a minister of God, an avenger for wrath to him that doeth evil."

Therefore obedience must be rendered to rulers not only as a matter of prudence but also as a matter of conscience, not only because it is dangerous to resist but also because it is right to submit to the representatives of God. We recognize this principle of the divine right of the state when we pay taxes for the support of its functions; as Paul declares, "For this cause ye pay tribute also; for they are ministers of God's service." Therefore Paul concludes his exhortation and prepares the way for the next paragraph by a general injunction which covers all the duties upon which he has been dwelling, "Render to all their dues"; and he specifies four forms of such dues which have been interpreted as follows: "tribute" even to a foreign superior power; "custom" for government support; "fear" or respectful awe for one in power; "honor" paid to a ruler.

Therefore, the important principles of Christian citizenship set forth in this paragraph include the conceptions that one has obligations to the state in addition to his obligations to the church; that human government is a divine institution; that its purpose is beneficent, two of its main functions being to protect and help those who do right and to restrain and punish evildoers; and therefore that loyalty to civil authorities is the duty of every follower of Christ.

In this connection, however, several observations should be made:

First, no particular form of government is hereby commended or advocated by the apostle. Almost any form is better than anarchy, and insofar is worthy of loyal support.

Second, loyalty does not preclude endeavors to improve a government; nor does it forbid one from raising the question as to whether a particular officer or group of officers rightly represents a government. There is such a thing as the divine right of the state, but there is also a divine right of revolution. Paul, however, is stating a general principle for normal conditions.

Third, one must be loyal to the government even in spite of the character of the civil rulers, who may be selfish, arbitrary, oppressive, and immoral men. Paul urged loyalty to Nero. The Roman government was a benefit to mankind in spite of the Caesars.

Fourth, one must not disobey conscience in submitting to civil government. Without being a rebel he can refuse to do what he regards as wrong, but he must patiently endure the penalty.

Fifth, while duties to the church are distinct from duties to the state, the performance of either is equally binding upon a Christian. The payment of a tax may be as real an expression of spiritual life as the offering of a public prayer.

## 2. THE ANIMATING PRINCIPLE OF LOVE
### Ch. 13:8-10

*8 Owe no man anything, save to love one another: for he that loveth his neighbor hath fulfilled the law. 9 For this, Thou shalt not commit adultery, Thou shalt not kill, Thou shalt not steal, Thou shalt not covet, and if there be any other commandment, it is summed up in this word, namely, Thou shalt love thy neighbor as thyself. 10 Love worketh no ill to his neighbor: love therefore is the fulfilment of the law.*

After insisting upon loyalty to the officials of the state, Paul proceeds to enforce the principle of love, which must control the relations of a Christian toward all his fellow citizens in the state. He has been saying that one must pay every lawful obligation to the government; he now reminds his readers that one must also pay every just debt to his neighbor; but that there is one obligation which he must continue paying, even though it can never be discharged fully, namely, the debt of love. "Owe no man anything, save to love one another."

The reason why love is of so great importance consists in the fact that love is the fulfillment of all law, and law is the very foundation of the state. Paul has just shown that no Christian is exempt from loyalty; he is declaring that one who loves his neighbor will not injure his neighbor, but will fulfill toward him all that the law demands. One who loves will not borrow from a neighbor that which he cannot repay; he will not wrong his neighbor by adultery, theft, murder, or covetousness. In fact, all special precepts are summarized in that of love; so that love becomes for a Christian the great principle which takes the place of law, and yet which makes possible the fulfillment of law.   So it is that every conceivable moral requirement is summed up in this one New Testament commandment, "Thou shalt love thy neighbor as thyself."   It is evident, then, that if one has the same regard for the welfare and happiness of his neighbor as he has toward his own, he will work "no ill to his neighbor"; he will fulfill inevitably all that the law requires and all that love demands.

### 3. THE PURIFYING MOTIVE OF HOPE
### Ch. 13:11-14

*11 And this, knowing the season, that already it is time for you to awake out of sleep: for now is salvation nearer to us than when we* first *believed.   12 The night is far spent, and the day is at hand: let us therefore cast off the works of darkness, and let us put on the armor of light. 13 Let us walk becomingly, as in the day; not in revelling and drunkenness, not in chambering and wantonness, not in strife and jealousy.   14 But put ye on the Lord Jesus Christ, and make not provision for the flesh, to* fulfil *the lusts* thereof.

To enforce the duties on which he has been dwelling the apostle now appeals to the hope of the completed salvation which Christians are to enjoy at the return of Christ: "And this [do]," particularly this continual paying of the debt of love, "knowing [as you do] the season," the definite period marked out by the Master as preceding his return, "that already it is time for you to awake out of sleep."

In view of the coming of the Lord, the readers are exhorted to arouse themselves from all spiritual indifference because their perfected salvation, when they are to be glorified with Christ, is nearer than when they first believed on him.   Paul seems to borrow his figures of speech from the actions of a Roman soldier who, as the dawn approached, awoke from slumber, laid aside the garments in which he had been sleeping, put on his gleaming armor, and stepped forth gladly to greet the day. Paul declares that his readers should regard the night of their distress and sorrow as nearly passed and the day of their deliverance and glory as about to dawn. They should cast off the deeds and habits which belong to the unbelieving world and to the kingdom of darkness. They should put on the bright armor of the Christian soldier, the matchless "armor of God." They should go forth to walk worthily of their heavenly calling. Avoiding all intemperance, impurity, and unkindness, they should identify themselves wholly with Christ in every purpose and act, putting on his perfectness of character, and making no provision for gratifying the sensual desires and appetites by which they were formerly controlled. They should so live that with gladness they could greet their returning Lord.

## C. QUESTIONS OF CONSCIENCE
### Chs. 14:1 to 15:13

### 1. DO NOT JUDGE OTHERS  Ch. 14:1-12

*1 But him that is weak in faith receive ye, yet not for decision of scruples. 2 One man hath faith to eat all things: but he that is weak eateth herbs. 3 Let not him that eateth set at nought him that eateth not; and let not him that eateth not judge him that eateth: for God hath received him. 4 Who art thou that judgest the servant of another? to his own lord he standeth or falleth. Yea, he shall be made to stand; for the Lord hath power to make him stand. 5 One man esteemeth one day above another: another esteemeth every day alike. Let each man be fully assured in his own mind. 6 He that regardeth the day, regardeth it unto the Lord: and he that eateth, eateth unto the Lord, for he giveth God thanks; and he that eateth not, unto the Lord he eateth not, and giveth God thanks. 7 For none of us liveth to himself, and none dieth to himself. 8 For whether we live, we live unto the Lord; or whether we die, we die unto the Lord: whether we live therefore, or die, we are the Lord's. 9 For to this end Christ died and*

*lived* again, *that he might be Lord of both the dead and
the living. 10 But thou, why dost thou judge thy brother?
or thou again, why dost thou set at nought thy brother?
for we shall all stand before the judgment-seat of God.
11 For it is written,*

> *As I live, saith the Lord, to me every knee shall bow,
> And every tongue shall confess to God.*

*12 So then each one of us shall give account of himself to
God.*

Some things are unquestionably right, and others are
as unquestionably wrong, but there are still others as to
which the consciences of men differ. These "questions of
conscience" arise among Christians and become the
sources of serious trouble. Christians who are overscrupulous are apt to condemn others as lax or "inconsistent,"
while those who feel no scruples as to the practices in question are tempted to despise their fellow Christians as
bigoted or fanatical or narrow.

As to these questions which concern matters morally
indifferent, Paul lays down three great principles: Do not
judge others (ch. 14:1-12); do not tempt others (vs.
13-23); follow Christ's example of forbearance and love
(ch. 15:1-13).

One "that is weak in faith," who does not grasp the
full meaning of salvation by grace, who thinks that his
keeping certain rules as to food or religious rites will make
him more acceptable to God, is to be received into the
church, but is not to be argued with as to his scruples.
(V. 1.) One man may understand that eating or refraining from certain wholesome foods is a matter of moral indifference; another man may believe that he will be more
pleasing to God if he eats only vegetables. (V. 2.)

However, neither is to judge the other. The one who
eats foods of all kinds is not to despise the other; and the
one who eats only vegetables is not to condemn the first,
but to remember that God has received him as his servant,
and therefore, as it would be improper to intrude into the

household affairs of another person and to pass judgment
upon his servants, so we as Christians are not to pass
judgment upon our fellow Christians, who are not our
servants but are servants of God. Each one is responsible
to his Lord, and the overscrupulous brother must feel no
anxiety for the one who indulges in food from which he
himself refrains. His Lord will keep the less scrupulous
brother from falling and not allow his innocent indulgence
to prove for him a fatal snare. (Vs. 3-4.)

So, too, one man regards certain days as particularly
holy, while another regards all days alike, excepting of
course the Sabbath Day. There is no exact rule as to the
observance of such "holy" days, or holidays. Each one
must be certain as to what he regards to be right. He must
do what he thinks will please his Master. Whether in
keeping holy days or in partaking or refraining from food,
his actions must be regulated by this great principle of the
lordship of Christ. Whether living or dying we recognize
him as Lord, and belong to him, who by his dying for us
and by his living again has become the Lord of the dead
and the living. (Vs. 5-9.)

Why, then, should one of us condemn his brother as lax
and inconsistent, or why should another of us despise his
brother as narrow and bigoted, since we all are to stand
before the divine judgment seat, as indeed Isaiah predicted: "As I live, saith the Lord, to me every knee shall
bow." Let us, therefore, as fellow Christians, servants of
the same Lord, refrain from judging one another, particularly in matters of moral indifference, since "each one of
us shall give account of himself to God." (Vs. 10-12).

### 2. DO NOT TEMPT OTHERS   Ch. 14:13-23

*13 Let us not therefore judge one another any more: but
judge ye this rather, that no man put a stumblingblock in
his brother's way, or an occasion of falling. 14 I know,
and am persuaded in the Lord Jesus, that nothing is un-*

*clean of itself: save that to him who accounteth anything
to be unclean, to him it is unclean.   15 For if because of
meat thy brother is grieved, thou walkest no longer in love.
Destroy not with thy meat him for whom Christ died.   16
Let not then your good be evil spoken of:   17 for the kingdom of God is not eating and drinking, but righteousness
and peace and joy in the Holy Spirit.   18 For he that
herein serveth Christ is well-pleasing to God, and approved
of men.   19 So then let us follow after things which make
for peace, and things whereby we may edify one another.
20 Overthrow not for meat's sake the work of God.   All
things indeed are clean; howbeit it is evil for that man who
eateth with offence.   21 It is good not to eat flesh, nor to
drink wine, nor to do anything whereby thy brother stumbleth.   22 The faith which thou hast, have thou to thyself
before God.   Happy is he that judgeth not himself in that
which he approveth.   23 But he that doubteth is condemned if he eat, because he eateth not of faith; and whatsoever is not of faith is sin.*

It has just been shown that we are not to despise or to
condemn others for their attitude toward things which are
morally indifferent, such as the eating of various kinds of
food or the observance of certain days as holy.   On the
other hand, as Paul teaches in this paragraph, we must
have a due regard for the consciences and the convictions
of others.   We may feel certain that for us a certain practice is quite innocent, yet we may conclude that it is wise
for us to give it up, lest it may offend others or lead them
to do what their own consciences forbid.   We have the
right to do anything which we believe to be innocent; yet
the greatest right is that of relinquishing a right for the
sake of others.   Even indulgence which in itself may not
be wrong may be sinful if it causes others distress or if it
leads others astray.   Such, in substance, is the message
which Paul here presents.   (Vs. 13-23).

In view of the future judgment of God, let us not judge
one another, but rather let it be our determination that
we shall put nothing in the way of a brother which will

make him stumble or fall.   (V. 13.)

It is true that the old ceremonial distinctions between clean and unclean foods are no longer in force; but if a man does not understand this and regards certain food as "unclean," then, so far as his conscience is concerned, that food is unclean and he does wrong to partake of it. If then he sees you eat such food, and is thus led to do the same, you may be leading him into sin and may be destroying one "for whom Christ died." (Vs. 14-15.) Christian liberty and your freedom from scruples may become an occasion for reproach in leading others to do what they regard as wrong.

It is not important that you should eat and drink everything that you desire and that you regard as right; self-denial for the sake of others may be far more necessary. In "the kingdom of God" the essential things are not "eating and drinking"; these are relatively trivial and insignificant; the important things are "righteousness" in our relations to others, and the "peace and joy" which result from true spiritual fellowship. A life lived with these essential Christian realities in view will be "well-pleasing to God, and approved of men." (Vs. 16-18.)

So, then, in these comparatively unimportant matters, let us determine our actions by doing what will make for peace and will be helpful to others. Merely for the sake of eating some kind of food which we prefer, or indulging in some questionable practice which we regard as harmless, we should not "overthrow" the work of grace which God has begun in the soul of some more scrupulous brother; for while the matter in question may be morally indifferent, it is really wrong for the one who regards it as wrong and who violates his consciences by doing the very thing you regard as innocent. (Vs. 19-20.)

The great rule, therefore, is this, whatever self-sacrifice may be involved: "It is good not to eat flesh, nor to drink wine, nor to do anything whereby thy brother stumbleth." (V. 21.)

If one has such a clear conviction of Christian truth that he is free from all unnecessary scruples, he should not make a display of his conscious liberty, particularly not in such a way as to offend or tempt a weaker or less intelligent brother. He should cherish such faith alone with God. Happy is the man who feels no rebuke of conscience when indulging in those practices as to which the consciences of Christians definitely differ. (V. 22.)

On the other hand, if one is troubled by scruples, and doubts whether it is right for him to do what he sees other Christians doing, then weakly to comply with such others is to incur condemnation; for his act does not result from faith in Christ and from an intelligent knowledge of the freedom which true faith secures; he is doing what he thinks may be morally wrong; and anything which we do not believe to be morally right is sinful. (V. 23.)

Thus Paul warns us that we may tempt others to sin even when we are doing something which we regard as innocent; and that, on the other hand, we may sin in doing that which others regard as harmless but which our own consciences do not heartily approve.

### 3. Follow the Example of Christ  Ch. 15:1-13

*1 Now we that are strong ought to bear the infirmities of the weak, and not to please ourselves. 2 Let each one of us please his neighbor for that which is good, unto edifying. 3 For Christ also pleased not himself; but, as it is written, The reproaches of them that reproached thee fell upon me. 4 For whatsoever things were written aforetime were written for our learning, that through patience and through comfort of the scriptures we might have hope. 5 Now the God of patience and of comfort grant you to be of the same mind one with another according to Christ Jesus: 6 that with one accord ye may with one mouth glorify the God and Father of our Lord Jesus Christ. 7 Wherefore receive ye one another, even as Christ also received you, to the glory of God. 8 For I say that Christ hath been made a minister of the circumcision for the truth of God, that he might confirm the promises given unto the fathers, 9 and that the Gentiles might glorify God for his mercy; as it is written,*

> *Therefore will I give praise unto thee among the Gentiles,*
> *And sing unto thy name.*

*10 And again he saith,*

> *Rejoice, ye Gentiles, with his people.*

*11 And again,*

> *Praise the Lord, all ye Gentiles;*
> *And let all the peoples praise him.*

*12 And again, Isaiah saith,*

> *There shall be the root of Jesse,*
> *And he that ariseth to rule over the Gentiles;*
> *On him shall the Gentiles hope.*

*13 Now the God of hope fill you with all joy and peace in believing, that ye may abound in hope, in the power of the Holy Spirit.*

Paul is still considering the two classes into which Christians are divided by questions of conscience, that is, by their attitude toward matters which, while not in themselves sinful, are regarded by one class as right and by another class as wrong. There are those who are "weak" or defective in faith, who consequently magnify ritual requirements into moral obligations; or, they look upon pleasures as sinful; or, they believe they can make themselves more acceptable to God by denying themselves things absolutely innocent.

In the preceding chapter the apostle has urged the "weak" not to condemn the strong, and the "strong" not to tempt or needlessly offend the "weak." Here he enjoins both classes to show mutual forbearance and love, following the example of Christ as set forth in the Scriptures, that all may be united in harmonious praise. Thus, too, should be brought together the two great divisions of the church, the Jew and the Gentile. Christ has received both; they should receive each other and await in joyous confidence the consummation of their glorious hopes in Christ.

"Now we that are strong ought to bear the infirmities of the weak," of those whose faith is defective, of those who are overscrupulous and narrow, and bigoted and childish. We ought "not to please ourselves," but to please each one his neighbor with a view to his moral good and his spiritual growth. Our great Exemplar, Christ, "pleased not himself," but endured the greatest abuse and unkindness from the most bigoted and unreasonable men; as we read in the Scriptures, "The reproaches of them that reproached thee fell upon me."

The purpose of the Scripture is to give us instruction and so make us patient and hopeful. May God grant that all who have differences in the church may follow the example of Christ and so manifest his spirit that with "one accord" they may "glorify the God and Father of our Lord Jesus Christ"!

Therefore, whatever may divide us, even though some are Jews and some Gentiles, let us receive one another as Christ received us. He came to show to the Jews the fidelity of God to his promises, and to show to the Gentiles the wonders of his grace, as passage after passage in the Old Testament shows. We surely should be ready to live in unity as members of the great body of the redeemed, for the very purpose of God was to unite all peoples in one great harmony of praise to his goodness and mercy in Christ Jesus. May the God of all hope grant that our faith may issue in a life of such joy and peace that by the power of the Holy Spirit we "may abound in hope"!

# IV
# THE CONCLUSION
Chs. 15:14 to 16:27

## A. PAUL'S REASONS FOR WRITING
### Ch. 15:14-21

*14 And I myself also am persuaded of you, my brethren, that ye yourselves are full of goodness, filled with all knowledge, able also to admonish one another. 15 But I write the more boldly unto you in some measure, as putting you again in remembrance, because of the grace that was given me of God, 16 that I should be a minister of Christ Jesus unto the Gentiles, ministering the gospel of God, that the offering up of the Gentiles might be made acceptable, being sanctified by the Holy Spirit. 17 I have therefore my glorying in Christ Jesus in things pertaining to God. 18 For I will not dare to speak of any things save those which Christ wrought through me, for the obedience of the Gentiles, by word and deed, 19 in the power of signs and wonders, in the power of the Holy Spirit; so that from Jerusalem, and round about even unto Illyricum, I have fully preached the gospel of Christ; 20 yea, making it my aim so to preach the gospel, not where Christ was already named, that I might not build upon another man's foundation; 21 but, as it is written,*

> *They shall see, to whom no tidings of him came,*
> *And they who have not heard shall understand.*

In bringing his epistle to a close, Paul first gives his reasons for writing to the Romans. This he does with notable courtesy and modesty and tact. He has written not because of any particular lack on their part but because of his special interest in them, since he is the apostle to the Gentiles and naturally has upon his heart the Christians who are living in the great imperial capital of the Gentile world.

He is persuaded that they are "full of goodness" and well instructed in the gospel and so quite capable of admonishing one another. Nevertheless he has written, even with considerable boldness and frankness, not so much to tell them new truths as to remind them of those they had already received. With such humility does Paul refer to a letter which sets forth with inspired impressiveness the most profound truths ever entertained by the human mind. He explains that he has made bold to write these truths to them because God has appointed him to be "a minister of Christ Jesus unto the Gentiles." This ministry Paul describes in figures borrowed from the Jewish ritual. Preaching the gospel is his priestly service, and its great purpose is that Gentile believers will be so transformed by its power that they will become an offering which he can present, acceptable to God, "being sanctified by the Holy Spirit."

This ministry, as exercised by Paul, is a just ground of pride, although he gives all the glory to Christ. He has been widely used in bringing Gentiles to obey God, his "word and deed" having been attested by miraculous "signs and wonders" wrought by the Holy Spirit, so that he had "fully preached the gospel of Christ," from Jerusalem to Illyricum, on the west of Macedonia. His one great purpose, his point of honor, his ambition, ever had been to preach the gospel where Christ had not been named, that he "might not build upon another man's foundation"; and he describes this aim in words borrowed from Isaiah when picturing the astonishment of the nations as they learn of the suffering Servant of Jehovah:

"They shall see, to whom no tidings of him came,
And they who have not heard shall understand."

## B. PAUL'S PERSONAL PLANS    Ch. 15:22-33

*22 Wherefore also I was hindered these many times from coming to you: 23 but now, having no more any place in these regions, and having these many years a long-ing to come unto you, 24 whensoever I go unto Spain (for I hope to see you in my journey, and to be brought on my way thitherward by you, if first in some measure I shall have been satisfied with your company)—25 but now, I say, I go unto Jerusalem, ministering unto the saints. 26 For it hath been the good pleasure of Macedonia and Achaia to make a certain contribution for the poor among the saints that are at Jerusalem. 27 Yea, it hath been their good pleasure; and their debtors they are. For if the Gen-tiles have been made partakers of their spiritual things, they owe it to them also to minister unto them in carnal things. 28 When therefore I have accomplished this, and have sealed to them this fruit, I will go on by you unto Spain. 29 And I know that, when I come unto you, I shall come in the fulness of the blessing of Christ.*

*30 Now I beseech you, brethren, by our Lord Jesus Christ, and by the love of the Spirit, that ye strive together with me in your prayers to God for me; 31 that I may be delivered from them that are disobedient in Judæa, and that my ministration which I have for Jerusalem may be ac-ceptable to the saints; 32 that I may come unto you in joy through the will of God, and together with you find rest. 33 Now the God of peace be with you all. Amen.*

Paul has been glorying in the ministry which is his as the chosen apostle to the Gentiles; but he realizes that, in spite of its wide scope, its labors are comparatively unful-filled; he always had his eyes fixed on "the regions be-yond," and he proceeds to tell his friends in Rome of his wide-reaching plans. Their city, the great imperial capi-tal, has for years been the goal of his ambition. However, he has been hindered from coming to them hitherto by his work in regions farther east; but now this work is so far completed that he can carry out a long-cherished purpose of preaching the gospel in Spain, and on the way he will visit Rome and enjoy the spiritual refreshment of fellow-ship with the friends to whom he is writing, and by them be helped forward on his journey to the West.

First, however, he must go in exactly the opposite direction; he must start eastward to carry relief to the needy Christians in Jerusalem. He is taking a "certain contribution" from the churches of Macedonia and Achaia. It had been a voluntary offering made with pleasure, yet it was, in a sense, the payment of a debt, for the Gentile churches owed to the Christians in Jerusalem all their spiritual blessings, and they could meet this indebtedness only by ministering to them in things temporal. In this offering, Paul had shown the deepest interest, not only because he had promised such aid and because it was to relieve his own fellow countrymen, but also because such an expression of charity would help to bind together Jews and Gentiles into one sympathetic body.

When Paul has fulfilled this mission, he promises to come to Rome and to pass onward to Spain. He feels assured that his coming will result in a special manifestation of grace: he will come "in the fulness of the blessing of Christ."

Paul realizes, however, the perils and the difficulties which await him, and therefore he closes this outline of his personal plans with an earnest request that the Roman Christians will unite in prayers on his behalf. He beseeches them by the Lord Jesus Christ, and by the brotherly love which his Spirit inspires in believers, that they will unite with him "in an intense energy of prayer" that he may be delivered from the unbelieving Jews, who were always his bitterest foes, and also that the peace offering of the Gentile churches may prove acceptable to the Jewish Christians of whose narrow prejudices Paul was well aware. Should these united prayers be answered, then Paul would come to his Roman friends with joy and find rest and refreshment in their fellowship. To this request for prayer Paul adds a petition of his own. In its mention of "peace" it sounds a keynote of the epistle, it voices a deep yearning of every heart: "Now the God of peace be with you all. Amen."

## C. THE COMMENDATION OF PHOEBE
### Ch. 16:1-2

*1 I commend unto you Phœbe our sister, who is a servant of the church that is at Cenchreæ: 2 that ye receive her in the Lord, worthily of the saints, and that ye assist her in whatsoever matter she may have need of you: for she herself also hath been a helper of many, and of mine own self.*

It has been commonly assumed that Phoebe was the bearer of this letter from Corinth to Rome. There is nothing to prove this, as no other mention of Phoebe is made elsewhere; but it properly has been called "a supposition which there is nothing to contradict."

Even more uncertain is the assumption that Phoebe was a deaconess. It is true that this office was established in the Christian church at a rather early date, but the word translated "servant," sometimes rendered "deaconess," may denote merely the charity and hospitality which should characterize the life of every true Christian and which seem to have been exhibited by Phoebe in a marked degree.

She was a member of the church at Cenchreae, the port of Corinth, nine miles east of that city. The apostle officially "commends" or introduces her to the church at Rome, urging that she be received "in the Lord" and in a manner worthy of Christians, implying not only that her needs be supplied but also that she be granted every spiritual privilege. Furthermore, Paul bespeaks for her assistance in whatsoever matter she may have need, possibly indicating that she was going to Rome on business in which they could afford her special help.

This cordial commendation was given in view of the fact that Phoebe had "been a helper of many" and of Paul himself. The term "helper" is almost the same as "patroness" and intimates that the one so designated was possibly a person of some wealth and social position. Just how this woman had befriended Paul and his fellow Christians is not stated, but surely his courteous and gracious commendation has given to her a place of imperishable fame.

## D. PAUL'S GREETINGS TO THE ROMANS
### Ch. 16:3-16

*3 Salute Prisca and Aquila my fellow-workers in Christ Jesus, 4 who for my life laid down their own necks; unto whom not only I give thanks, but also all the churches of the Gentiles: 5 and salute the church that is in their house. Salute Epænetus my beloved, who is the firstfruits of Asia unto Christ. 6 Salute Mary, who bestowed much labor on you. 7 Salute Andronicus and Junias, my kinsmen, and my fellow-prisoners, who are of note among the apostles, who also have been in Christ before me. 8 Salute Ampliatus my beloved in the Lord. 9 Salute Urbanus our fellow-worker in Christ, and Stachys my beloved. 10 Salute Apelles the approved in Christ. Salute them that are of the household of Aristobulus. 11 Salute Herodion my kinsman. Salute them of the household of Narcissus, that are in the Lord. 12 Salute Tryphæna and Tryphosa, who labor in the Lord. Salute Persis the beloved, who labored much in the Lord. 13 Salute Rufus the chosen in the Lord, and his mother and mine. 14 Salute Asyncritus, Phlegon, Hermes, Patrobas, Hermas, and the brethren that are with them. 15 Salute Philologus and Julia, Nereus and his sister, and Olympas, and all the saints that are with them. 16 Salute one another with a holy kiss. All the churches of Christ salute you.*

This list of obscure names is of great value and of true significance. It gives an aspect of reality and deep human interest to the whole epistle, and its accompanying phrases indicate that Christian doctrines were bearing fruit in the lives of those to whom they had been proclaimed.

These greetings reveal the heart of Paul, showing his

tender affection, his appreciation of kindness, his warm sympathy, and his high valuation of human friendships. They give instructive glimpses of the life of the early church, enabling us to form a picture of its close fellowships, its heroic sufferings, its generous sympathies, its purity, its devotion, its faith, its hope, its love.

Of all these names the only ones which are familiar are those of Prisca and Aquila, the friends with whom Paul had lived in Corinth who more recently seem to have saved the life of Paul at great hazard, for his sake having "laid down their own necks." They were only tentmakers, but their wide travel and their intelligent testimony for Christ made them deserving of thanks from "all the churches of the Gentiles." To them Paul sends his greeting, and also to the believers in Rome who met at their home for Christian worship.

The rest of the names here mentioned appear in no other place. Most of them seem to be those of slaves or freedmen; but these men and women, not recognized by the world, have attained glory enough by being known through all the passing centuries as friends of Paul and followers of Christ.

The apostle closes his salutation to the Christians in Rome by urging them to "salute one another with a holy kiss." It was an Oriental and particularly a Jewish custom to combine a kiss with a greeting; here, however, Paul does not mean merely a token of friendship: nor yet is he establishing "the kiss of peace" as a permanent ordinance or regular part of the Christian religious service. He only intended that, when his letter had been heard and his salutations received, they should greet one another as fellow members of the church.

When Paul now adds, "All the churches of Christ salute you," he is using a general expression; however, he indicates his wide acquaintance with the churches, and the deep interest which all felt in the welfare of the church at Rome.

## E. A WARNING AGAINST FALSE TEACHERS
### Ch. 16:17-20

*17 Now I beseech you, brethren, mark them that are causing the divisions and occasions of stumbling, contrary to the doctrine which ye learned: and turn away from them. 18 For they that are such serve not our Lord Christ, but their own belly; and by their smooth and fair speech they beguile the hearts of the innocent. 19 For your obedience is come abroad unto all men. I rejoice therefore over you: but I would have you wise unto that which is good, and simple unto that which is evil. 20 And the God of peace shall bruise Satan under your feet shortly.*

*The grace of our Lord Jesus Christ be with you.*

It is not unnatural, as the epistle is brought to a close, and just after Paul has referred to the other Christian churches, that he should add a solemn warning against false teachers. He remembers what subtle and corrupting heresies have appeared among other bodies of believers, and he fears lest they may cause divisions and scandals among the Christians at Rome. He therefore urges his readers to "mark" and avoid such as may attempt to teach doctrines contrary to the gospel as it has been received by the Romans and as it has been set forth with such fullness and power in this epistle.

From such teachers Christians are to "turn away," because instead of being servants of Christ such are servants of their own appetites and of their own selfish interests, and by their plausible and flattering speech they are able to deceive the hearts of the guileless and unwary. From the pestilent influence of such teachers the Roman Christians were still free. The fame of their loyalty was everywhere reported. Therefore Paul rejoices over them; nevertheless he is anxious, and he is desirous that "their moral intelligence should not be impaired in the least by any dealings with evil," but that they might be "experts in good and innocents in evil."

False teachers, whom as the agents of evil Paul identifies with Satan, may come and cause dissensions, but soon, by the Spirit of God, victory will be secured and peace restored; at least, this seems to be the meaning of Paul's promise, "And the God of peace shall bruise Satan under your feet shortly."

So Paul closes this warning with a benediction: "The grace of our Lord Jesus Christ be with you."

## F. GREETINGS FROM PAUL'S COMPANIONS
Ch. 16:21-23

*21 Timothy my fellow-worker saluteth you; and Lucius and Jason and Sosipater, my kinsmen. 22 I Tertius, who write the epistle, salute you in the Lord. 23 Gaius my host, and of the whole church, saluteth you. Erastus the treasurer of the city saluteth you, and Quartus the brother.*

The letter seems to come to a close with the preceding paragraph, but now are added these salutations from Paul's friends and companions. It has been suggested that the letter, before being sent to Rome, was first read at a Christian gathering in Corinth, and that the greetings to the Roman church were appended at the request of these who are named.

First among them is Timothy, Paul's beloved "fellow-worker," his "child in the faith," his comrade on perilous journeys, his comfort in long imprisonments, and his deputy on difficult missions—a man who, as few others, knew the fullness and joy of the apostle's affection and love.

Lucius and Jason and Sosipater are difficult to identify; but Paul calls them his kinsmen, meaning probably his fellow countrymen, men who were of Jewish birth. Tertius, the amanuensis, by whom the letter is being written, adds his own greeting.

Then Gaius is mentioned, one who was at the time the host of the apostle; him Paul describes as being the host "of the whole church," meaning either that the Christians were wont to meet in his house for worship or that he extended his hospitality to all Christians who came as strangers to Corinth.

Erastus, the city treasurer, sends his greeting, together with that of Quartus, whom Paul designates "the brother." That an official holding so important a position as that of treasurer in the great city of Corinth was numbered among the Christian brotherhood shows that some men of prominence and power were members of that church in which Paul declared that there were "not many mighty" and "not many noble."

## G. THE DOXOLOGY Ch. 16:25-27

*25 Now to him that is able to establish you according to my gospel and the preaching of Jesus Christ, according to the revelation of the mystery which hath been kept in silence through times eternal, 26 but now is manifested, and by the scriptures of the prophets, according to the commandment of the eternal God, is made known unto all the nations unto obedience of faith: 27 to the only wise God, through Jesus Christ, to whom be the glory for ever. Amen.*

While Paul has given us many other superb doxologies, they are found in the body and not at the conclusion of his letters. This magnificent ascription of praise sums up the great thoughts of the epistle and is in perfect harmony with its contents. In particular, it should be noted how this closing paragraph reechoes the notes sounded in the opening verses of the epistle and repeats their significant phrases, thus pointing backward to what has been written, as the introduction in so large measure points forward to all that is to follow.

Paul ascribes praise to God who "is able to establish" the Roman Christians. In the opening of the epistle (ch. 1:11) he expresses a hope that they may be established by the imparting of some spiritual gift through his proposed ministry in Rome. Here he expresses the truth that nothing that man can do, not even the production of such an epistle as this, can in itself effect such a result. Only God can establish believers in their faith so that they cannot be moved.

This establishment is to take place in agreement with the gospel which Paul preached, a gospel of grace, a gospel of free salvation for all men through faith in Jesus Christ. The very sum and substance of this gospel is "the preaching of Jesus Christ," who is ever presented as the object of faith, the source of hope and life. This preaching of Christ sets forth the gracious purpose of God for the redemption of the world.

It is therefore in accordance with the revelation of that "mystery" which has been hidden in silence since the world began, but now has been disclosed. It is in perfect accord with the writings of the inspired prophets; and now by God's commandment it is proclaimed "unto all the nations" to bring them into the obedience of faith. To him who in such a saving purpose and in all his works of providence and grace shows himself "the only wise God," to him be "the glory for ever," through Jesus Christ. Amen.